Breaking the Word Barrier
Stories of Adults Learning to Read

BREAKING
the word BARRIER

Stories of Adults Learning to Read

Edited by MARILYN LERCH and ANGELA RANSON

GOOSE LANE

Edited by Paula Sarson.
Cover images: reader, stock.xchng.com, © Jenny Rollo; book pages, stock.xchnge.com.
Cover design and interior page design by Julie Scriver.
Printed in Canada on 100% PCW paper.
10 9 8 7 6 5 4 3 2 1

Library and Archives Canada Cataloguing in Publication

  Breaking the word barrier : stories of adults learning
to read / edited by Marilyn Lerch and Angela Ranson.

ISBN 978-0-86492-547-3

  1. Adult learning — Canada.   2. Literacy — Canada.
I. Lerch, Marilyn   II. Ranson, Angela, 1974-

LC5254.B69 2009   374'.01240971   C2009-903576-6

Goose Lane Editions acknowledges the financial support of the Canada Council for the Arts, the Government of Canada through the Book Publishing Industry Development Program (BPIDP), and the New Brunswick Department of Wellness, Culture, and Sport for its publishing activities.

Goose Lane Editions
Suite 330, 500 Beaverbrook Court
Fredericton, New Brunswick
CANADA E3B 5X4
www.gooselane.com

This book is dedicated to all the students
who walked the path to literacy
and to the mentors who accompanied them.

The following is a list of common acronyms found throughout the stories.

LLNB	Laubach Literacy New Brunswick
WFNB	Writers Federation of New Brunswick
GED	General Educational Development
NBCC	New Brunswick Community College
CALP	Community Adult Learning Program
SOUL	Speaking Out by Utilizing Learners
LCNB	Literacy Coalition of New Brunswick
TSD	Training & Skills Development program
ECE	Early Childhood Education

Contents

Reading Is Magic

This book is a tribute to courage. It is about ordinary people doing extraordinary things, about people who do not quit. Their stories are incredibly moving and their dedication to overcoming life's misfortunes is exemplary for all those who have been privileged, fortunate, or have had a much better hand dealt to them. Courage, generosity, and patience are the three most important virtues to survive the cynicism, greed, and frenzied times that we face. I see all of these qualities in the stories of these people, these tenacious people who decided to return to the deck and find the aces in order to start a new game with a winning hand. They are true inspirations, and this uplifting collection is a means for each of us to gain perspective on where we stand in our awareness of our access to information, education, and the gifts we have received, reading being one of the most important of all.

I have great admiration for the authors who were paired with the learners. Their attentive listening can be compared to the tutors who have worked with each learner and have been generous in sharing the keys to their own knowledge. Great stories need the talents of a storyteller to make them come alive. The writers have used their experience, style, and generosity to turn these testimonials into compassionate and engaging narratives.

Reading is a form of affection. It is an intimate moment of sharing information, a way of bonding around a story, a way of participating in the marvels of the imagination. For many of the adult learners in these stories, one of the most common incentives to reach their goal of literacy was the desire to read to their children, to help them with their homework.

Literacy is partly a family responsibility, and learning to read, to enjoy books, or to seek information in the printed word is often a habit that we learn by imitation within the family. Bedtime stories are a strong stimulus to plant a love for books in a child's young mind. Being deprived of such experiences in childhood can lead to the range of struggles later in life. The decision to work to achieve literacy in adulthood is often based on the perception that something important is missing, that an essential component of a balanced life has been lost.

When reading this collection, I have been intrigued by the opening and closing sentences and also by the narratives themselves, but as much as they are about overcoming some of life's most taxing moments, they are also stories with happy endings. The stories reflect the experiences of the writers, the impact that these meetings have had on their lives, and in turn, on ours, for the stories reveal to us a side of life that one might expect to encounter in fiction. Yet, these are not fictitious tales. They are real stories about real people living real lives. They are about people we meet every day — on the street, in supermarkets, at sports arenas, at Tim Horton's, or in convenience stores. They are our neighbours who silently carry a social stigma until they decide to act, until they meet someone they can trust and partner with to break the culture of defeat, someone like the Canadian Tire manager, who understood the destructive drama brooding in Raymond who recalls, "The boss told me he admired me for learning to read. He wanted to shake my hand," and as result he was able to get the Christmas present he wanted to give to his little girl.

I have participated in many literacy events, and I know well the importance of raising literacy skills. We need to work together — organizations, agencies, and the different levels of government — to create a common front. We are often asked to listen to someone who has walked the line, someone whose story could very well have been part of this book and, indeed, whose story turns out to be quite moving and motivating. Yet, most of the focus is placed on literacy skills in the classroom — based on the assumption, as I have heard someone remark, that we must act at an age when it is still possible to change the course of things.

Granted, we have to effect change at all levels, but we must never forget that illiteracy touches too many people beyond the classroom, and it is everyone's business to address it. Adult learners need our support now more than ever, for they are faced with difficulties that might turn into tragedies. Reading skills are among the most important solutions to such emotional and functional distress.

You might recall the slogan that was adopted by the United Negro College Fund in the 1970s: a mind is a terrible thing to waste. The mind, like the body, can be trained to perform amazing and complex operations, and like a high-performance athlete, artist, or visionary, it can be pushed to perform a high degree of accomplishment. But this does not happen overnight. The proper tools are needed to venture out on such a journey. One of the most basic components to building the mind is the ability to access, exchange, and produce information, usually contained in books, but accessible only by the ability to read, comprehend, and retain knowledge. The people, whose touching journeys are described in this book, have realized more than most the importance of such promises. They believed that reading could open a door in their lives and that beyond the cold, grey wall lies a path that could lead toward their dreams.

A mind is a terrible thing to waste indeed. In this small corner of the world where we are so very few, everyone is needed to be part of a winning team. Literacy is part of the game plan and its importance is measured and felt every day, every where, and with every one. This is a collective struggle and undoubtedly the solution must come from all of us. The people in this book have proven that a cycle of dependency can be broken, and their stories confirm that every contribution counts, every word learned is a victory, every sentence read enhances our collective consciousness.

Reading is a wonderful gift. We did not invent this system of communication. We are merely its inheritors, but we have the responsibility to share it, to add to it, and to transmit it to future generations. We live in an exciting age, in a wonderful country where education is free and where all children have access to the wonders of a civilization to which they will eventually contribute. This is the perfect script, at least on paper. However, reality is somehow slightly different. Granted, there has been a democratization of knowledge and access to the tools of learning, and there have been strong incentives to acquire the skills that seem so essential to the fulfillment and enjoyment of our heritage as humans. Why, then, do we continue to face a high rate of illiteracy? Why do we do not seem to find adequate solutions to a problem so pervasive that we hesitate to acknowledge its real consequences? The rate of illiteracy is so alarming that a new social contract is required to come to terms with it. We need to ask ourselves the real questions, and we need to find effective solutions.

This is a most inspiring collection of stories about real people who decided to win. Their personal victories will eventually turn out to be our collective triumph. They have ventured into another world, which happens to be their own, for reading expands skills and opens doors to a whole new life. As one of the learners reflects, "My new path leads to other doors that I'm sure will open on unimagined vistas of possibility." To open a book or a newspaper or a computer document is like opening the door to a world that we travel line after line, word to word on a path to greater knowledge, entertainment, and even enchantment.

Reading is magic for it transforms the world around us, and yes, it can also grant wishes. This book is a testimony to that power.

HERMÉNÉGILDE CHIASSON
Lieutenant-Governor of New Brunswick

Preface

Two years ago, Laubach Literacy New Brunswick (LLNB) and the Writers Federation of New Brunswick (WFNB) entered upon a joint project to promote literacy in our province. This endeavour was undertaken in response to the appalling literacy statistics revealed by the 1993 and 2003 International Adult Literacy and Skills Survey for New Brunswick. The result is *Breaking the Word Barrier: Stories of Adults Learning to Read.*

Seventeen members of the WFNB volunteered to interview seventeen adult students engaged in either literacy programs or academic upgrading classes. The students ranged in age from nineteen to seventy-one and came from cities, towns, and rural communities across New Brunswick. An estimated two hundred hours of interviews were conducted. This process empowered and enlightened students and writers.

Those struggling to read and write face many barriers, not the least of which is the stigma imposed by society — if you are not functionally literate, you are somehow inferior. Admitting that one needs help and seeking it under these conditions can be extremely difficult, and that is why we consider the seventeen students featured in this collection to be heroes. The narratives, crafted from the interviews, are a tribute to the students' courage and determination as they faced and overcame daunting challenges. We hope the joy they found in improving their literacy skills will inspire those who listen to or read *Breaking the Word Barrier*.

The heartfelt wish of all those who participated in the creation of this book is that it will encourage thousands of older youth and adults to seize the opportunities readily available and that it will draw the public's attention to the serious literacy deficit in New Brunswick.

Thanks must be given to Noeline Bridge and Angela Ranson, WFNB members who spent many hours working on the committee that established procedures and guidelines for the project. Ana Watts, Rhona Sawlor, and Cathy Fynn volunteered their editing services.

Without the generous donations from the Atlantic Lottery Corporation and the Province of New Brunswick the book would have remained a dream. Additional funding was gratefully received from the Greater Moncton Literacy Advisory Board, Legs for Literacy, Laubach Literacy New Brunswick, and the Moncton Regional Learning Council.

Finally, LLNB and the WFNB owe a debt of gratitude to Goose Lane Editions, to its publisher Susanne Alexander, managing editor Akoulina Connell, and editor Paula Sarson for bringing the dream to publication.

MARILYN LERCH, President, WFNB
PETER SAWYER, Board Member, LLNB

Breaking the Word Barrier
STORIES OF ADULTS LEARNING TO READ

The Word for Love
BETH POWNING

When Linda was fourteen she was in grade five, attending school in East Saint John. After school she walked almost two kilometres home to her grandparents' house. When she stepped into the kitchen one March afternoon, her grandmother snatched her lunch can. "Grampy's been asking for you all day. Quick, go upstairs," she said. Linda hurried to her grandfather's room. Fifteen minutes later, he had passed away.

After his death, Linda quit school to stay home and help her grandmother. She did not know how to read. Arithmetic was a mystery. She could write only her own name.

"I couldn't do it anymore. I wasn't learning anything," she later recalled.

Linda was born in Saint John in 1950. At the age of sixteen months, she fell down a flight of stairs. She went to the children's hospital in Toronto and then was sent to the Montreal Shriner's Hospital. She sustained head injuries and damage to her left arm and leg. The doctors told her parents that she had a fifty-fifty chance of survival. Her mother had a job that she didn't want to give up to look after a disabled child. Linda was sent to live with her grandparents.

Her grandmother was a minister's daughter from Nova Scotia. Her grandfather, from St. Martin's, was totally blind. Linda became his faithful attendant, even though she herself walked with a limp and had the use of only one hand. She helped him bank the house with sand. She helped him saw wood, haul coal, lug buckets of water. She led him by the hand, became his eyes. She adored her grandparents.

Linda learned as a young child that her mother had not wanted to care for her. Forever afterward, when her parents arrived on occasional visits, Linda refused to see them. She went across the street to her best friend's house and would not come home until she saw the car leave the driveway. The hurt and bitterness of abandonment set in at an early age.

She started grade one in a combined one/two class, with grades three/four and five/six in the same room. Aside from learning disabilities as a result of her accident, Linda missed months of school, since every six months she went to the Montreal Children's Hospital for surgeries on her arm and leg. The teacher did not have time to help her. She was put in the slow learners' class. The other children teased her and called her "stupid."

At home in the green house on the Old Black River Road, Linda lived as an only child, although she did have two brothers and three half-sisters. The house had a sun porch filled with her grandmother's plants, and she would lie there on sunny summer days or play on the baseball diamond or in the nearby fields. She did not have the escape of television or the companionship of children's books. Her grandmother occasionally read aloud to Linda and helped her with her lessons but was unable to teach her to read.

Linda missed her grandfather terribly. Although she loved her grandmother, she and her Grampy had been close. Not only did they love each other, but she had been his helpmate, and this had given her a sense of responsibility and independence. After his death, Linda's grandmother moved downstairs to a room off the kitchen, and Linda asked if she might move into the bigger bedroom that had been her grandparents'. She could feel her grandfather's presence there. At night, she lay in the warm bed, wrapped in the sense of someone who had loved her for who she was. Without the comfort of a bedtime book, she remembered — and imagined.

* * *

At eighteen, she was pregnant. Her grandmother counselled her to stay single and raise the baby at home, but Linda married and had three children. Those were hard years. Eventually, she left her husband and went on welfare. She learned to read a few words and struggled to fill out her own welfare papers. Usually she had to rely on her half-sister for help. In the grocery store, she could not read the labels on boxes and cans. Although she worried about the fact that there was diabetes and heart disease in the family, she did not know whether the foods she bought contained salt or sugar. At church, she could not follow the words in the program or on the board or in the songbook.

She didn't feel lonely, only embarrassed. She did not want people to know she couldn't read. "If they found out, they would say — shocked, fascinated — 'I didn't know you couldn't read!'" She hated having to ask for help. One of her most painful memories is that she could not read storybooks to her children.

She noticed that people loved books. "Books made me feel bad. I wanted to know what the words said." She would try to read, propping her damaged arm on the left-hand page and running the finger of her good hand along the first sentence. She would make up her own story as her finger travelled down the page. She would turn the page and resume running her finger along the black, lacy lines, murmuring her imaginary tale.

She raised three children and eventually had five grandchildren. It never crossed her mind that she could ever learn to read. She was shy and retiring, afraid to talk to people, especially afraid to speak up in public.

"'You won't amount to anything,' people told me. The more people told me that, I got it into my head that I was going to be stupid for the rest of my life."

Linda volunteered at the Salvation Army for ten years. One day, when she was fifty years old, the program director came into the kitchen with an intriguing invitation. "Would any of you people like to learn to read and write?"

Linda's first thought was, "I'm kind of old."

Her grandfather came to her often in her dreams. On that day, she heard his voice repeatedly urging her on, "Do it, Linda! Do it. Put your mind to it."

At the end of the day, she went to the director's office. "I'll give it a try."

She was assigned a tutor, Gwen. Going to her first lesson, she was nervous, thinking the teacher might be "cranky or strict." Gwen and Linda liked each other, and the lessons went well. At first, it was very difficult for Linda to link sounds with letters, but she thrived with one-on-one teaching. She persevered, worked hard, and did her homework. "I learned more from my tutor than I ever did in school." Starting with a grade three proficiency level, in four years she had progressed to a grade nine level.

Linda's life changed.

In the fall of 2008, Linda and I arrange to meet in a private room at the Saint John Free Public Library. I see a small woman sitting in the library foyer. We shake hands. We're the same age, the same height. We both have grandchildren. I sense that she's nervous and determined. I feel her courage. She sits at the end of the table, patient and eager. She is ready to tell me more of her story. She carries her good news like a gift that she wants to share.

As she talks, I begin to see two people. There's the grey-haired woman who sits before me, one arm as muscled as a man's. With this strong arm, she lifts and settles her other arm on the table, making herself comfortable. She waits for my questions, brave in her composure. Her face is grooved by pain, despair, love, loss. Her eyes lilt with an impish delight, and her laugh lifts my heart. Then, gradually, I see the child, a small girl who is self-confident and capable. This little girl tells her grandfather how high to lift his shovel, where to push his wheelbarrow. She tells him what she sees: a raft of geese, autumn leaves, a sunset. She has the strength of character to follow her feelings — to disappear at the sight of her parents' car, to watch through a window, waiting for them to leave. I see the little girl who is tough and honest at the start of her life's journey, when people are just beginning to tell her that she won't amount to anything, and she doesn't, yet, believe them.

This is Linda now. "I met one of those kids I went to school with. I said, 'Have you seen me?' He answered, 'You've been on TV. You've been on radio, in the newspaper.' I said, 'Now call me stupid. I'm not stupid anymore, am I?' He didn't say anything."

"I missed out on graduation." When she received her Learning Achievement Award, "The tears were just flowing down my cheeks, I felt so good about that." At home, on her wall next to a painting of the Last Supper, are her certificates. She lights up, telling me about them. "All lined up," she says, making a descriptive motion with her hand. She recounts how her youngest granddaughter looked at them and said, "That is *good*!"

She has her own library card. She is a spokesperson for Read Saint John. She talks to different groups, and, like the best public speakers, tailors what she says to each group. She was asked to speak at a ribbon-cutting ceremony at the opening of the New Readers Collection at the Saint John Free Public Library. She carries a banner for Read Saint John in the yearly United Way parade. She talks one-on-one to people who might be embarrassed to discuss their low literacy skills. She wants people to know that it's possible to learn to read and write at any age.

As Linda tells me her story, she continuously juxtaposes her reality now with how her life used to be. "I couldn't read," she says. Quickly, proudly, she adds, "I can read now. I can read my own mail. I can look in the phone book. I don't have to ask how to spell. I take out books from the library. I write in my journal every day."

I ask if I may feel the muscle in her right arm. She smiles, shrugs back her shoulders, squeezes her hand into a fist, and hints at her scrappiness on the playground. In a matter-of-fact way, she tells me that people ask her how she gets by with only one arm. How does she do her housework? Hang clothes on the line? "I show them," she says with offhand pride. She's learning to play pool one-handed. I picture her squinting, lining up her cue with one powerful arm, taking an unguided shot.

Watching her, I think how we all have to journey to find our own particular strengths. Many of us, especially girls of the 1950s, suffered from low self-esteem simply because we were female and had few women role models, but most of us, of whatever gender or generation, were encouraged rather than hindered.

Linda, however, faced one barrier after another. She does not dwell on her physical challenges and how they may have contributed to playground cruelty or perceived inability by teachers. She does not blame the teachers or the school system that failed her. She acknowledges her bitterness about having been abandoned by her parents but sees it as yet another challenge, saying that she is working hard to forgive. She laughs and sighs about the man she was married to, the years as a teenage mother, and the long struggle to bring up three children. These facts are like bedrock: the hard underpinnings. *There it is*, she seems to say. *That was then.*

I ask about her imagination. Since she couldn't read, did she make things up?

"When I was a child, I had a vivid imagination." Now that she can read, her ability to imagine may be extraordinary. She talks about reading the Bible. "In my mind, I go way back to when Jesus was born. And *I picture myself there*." She stares at me, intently, and a long minute passes. I sense that she is not seeing me but has gone to some other place: a cold night in Bethlehem, a mother in a cow stall, cradling a child.

She is thrilled with discovery. The world has opened up. She tells me about the first book she ever took out of the library. It was about Bill Cosby. As she read it, she imagined the TV show. "I wish I had a family like that . . ." Now she's embarking on a book about an eighteenth-century Lady Diane — the first Lady Di. "I'm still learning."

She is radiant with pride. "People said, 'We can see a lot of change in you.' Everybody's hugging me, and saying, 'Oh, you're doing a good job. You should be proud of yourself.'"

Her half-sister told her that up in Heaven, her grandparents are looking down, so proud of her that her grandfather is playing his fiddle.

We chat about what's next for her. She tells me about a man she's met who can't talk. "I'm learning sign language. I'm going to take a book out of the library about it." She shows me some hand signs. Goodbye. Hello. She clasps her arms around herself, the sign for love. She says, "This is the word 'love.'"

Digging Holes
MARILYN LERCH

Joe knows about digging holes. He has helped his stepfather dig many of them in cemeteries from Dorchester to Bayfield. He has learned to strap the caskets and lower them carefully into the graves. "I've become desensitized," he says. "It's just a job." He quickly apologizes, his consideration for the feelings of others shining forth. Then, a mischievous fleeting smile crosses his face as he tells of a casket not properly secured that tipped up and threw the corpse out. "It wasn't us that did it."

Joe has dug holes figuratively, too. He dropped out of school in grade nine at age fourteen, drifted a while, and now, just turned nineteen, he has begun his second year in the Community Adult Learning Program. "I don't think I have much of a story to tell." Joe isn't sure why he was chosen to be interviewed; however, his tutor says he is an inspiration. He is doing this for her.

Joe is of stocky build, his hair close cut, his cheeks ruddy and dimpled. In a certain light, Joe's eyes change from hazel to green — a handsome young man, working his way out of a hole. How did he get there? What string of events led him one day in grade nine to clean out his locker, tell the school receptionist he was not coming back, and walk away? We all carry certain memories close to the surface. A word, a fragrance, and they come fully into the light. Joe remembers. He was three. His father was about to hurt his mother, and he ran to try to help. He couldn't do anything, of course. His brother, eight years older, told him stories he was too young to remember that further fuelled his anger.

Years later, he saw his father sitting in a car. He went up and tapped on the window. The man did not turn his head. Helplessness may root as shame. Shame often grows as the weed of low self-worth.

Not in grade eight, though. Joe says that he and his best friend were "on top of the social pyramid." Their classmates looked up to them. "We'd collect change from kids who had paid for their lunch and give it to kids who had no lunch." Joe watches me scribble this on a yellow legal pad. "Don't write that as if it was noble. We didn't do it every day." I promise I won't, but I cannot help admiring how the word sits easily on his tongue. Noble.

Joe has a way of tapping his cellphone when he is about to make a serious point, and he looks off into space. "You know how you can tell which kids in a class are going to be picked on, right? There were three boys like that in our grade eight class." One had a serious illness and died. One was working in the woods, and he was killed by a falling tree. These losses still touch him. "I'm glad I never picked on them. I'd have regrets." There is nothing self-congratulatory in this statement, just an innocent affirmation of Joe's apparent natural goodness.

The third student turned up in the Adult Learning Centre. "I remember you from middle school," the young man told Joe, "because you said you would never hurt me."

Joe summarizes his schooling: "From grade one to grade five, I was the good little white kid, didn't disturb anyone. From grade six to grade eight, I was in the 'bad class,' and we were kept together all through middle school." Joe explains that six or seven of his classmates were troublemakers and kept things in an uproar. He quickly adds, "I wasn't one of them." He says he was self-conscious about his weight at that time, not pudgy, just bigger than most of the kids. "You know the only kid I ever hit? He tried to pull up my shirt, and I didn't want anyone to see my stomach."

The transition to high school was difficult, compounded by migraine headaches, which his mother also suffers from. He was overwhelmed by the big school, all the new people. "You know how it is, you get off the school bus, and you see a group of kids over here and a group over there and another group over there, all friends. And you don't fit in anywhere."

He was failing math and not doing well in English. He had never mastered the multiplication tables, and math became undecipherable. He was sure one of his teachers hated him. "I felt that no matter what I did, she'd fail me." He chuckles. "I had a fantasy that I would become a teacher and teach this woman's son and give him as hard a time as she was giving me." So rather than toughing it out, Joe dropped out.

A relative helped him get into a home-schooling program, but it was a disaster. For whatever reason, the program provided no supervision. His mother worked, and his stepfather often worked nights and had to sleep during the day. So each morning Joe would face a stack of books with no incentive to work alone.

Joe spent two years drifting. "I played video games and helped my stepfather once in a while."

He did take a job in a grocery store but quit after a few weeks. "I didn't need the money and wasn't getting anything out of the work." But there is something else going on here. Joe drops his usual quiet delivery, becomes agitated and talks with great feeling about how his folks work several jobs, how they've worked hard all their lives, struggling to stay out of debt. This is a hole he'd rather not fall into; he'd like a different life.

The kind of life he wants and has wanted since he was a boy is to be a member of the Canadian Army. "There's more opportunity to make a difference, and if you die, you're remembered somewhere." Then Joe says something that goes to the heart of what he longs for. "Not dying for the country, but being willing to die for the guy beside you and him for me." Here is a compassionate young man who yearns for a world where people take care of each other, where loyalty and comradeship are valued above all. He dreams of being the top shooter in his class, then moving up to sharpshooter and then becoming a sniper.

"Do you hunt?" I ask.

"I could never kill an animal."

"But you could be a sniper?"

Joe looks at me. "It depends. If the soldier is defending his country, then it might be hard for me."

When Joe was seventeen, his best friend, who was living in another town, moved in with Joe's family in order to complete his grade twelve year. "He was a constant reminder that I should be graduating with him." Joe called the recruiting office around this time but found out he was not eligible because he hadn't completed grade ten. He thought he would feel out of place if he enrolled in his old school, so his aunt found out about the Adult Learning Centre. Soon he was studying with a teacher whom he describes as caring and dedicated and who puts everyone before herself.

This is how Joe understands himself with an unflinching honesty. "I'm a visual learner. I see a commercial one time, and I can repeat the whole thing back." He admits he has trouble staying with anything, school or jobs. "I'm kind of lazy. I got a cheque for my birthday a month ago and haven't cashed it." He's not very eager to be out on his own, buying groceries, paying bills. "I'd probably order out all the time." That's why the army appeals to him. "The army will shape me up. I'll have to do what I'm told to do. I've always had low self-esteem," he offers. "I don't need anyone to beat up on me. I do that to myself."

During the course of our conversations together, Joe exhibits a wide-ranging curiosity and knowledge about the world, garnered mainly from the Internet and TV. He is a walking encyclopedia about military equipment. From 9/11 to the Illuminati (he's a bit of a conspiracy theorist), to chips in the palm containing personal information, to blood clot-eating robots, to the movie *Zeitgeist*, Joe's lively intelligence comes into play. He read somewhere that the Cuban army delivers food to the people. "Maybe there is a different way," he ponders. An older friend told him he's already old because he thinks and cares about what is going on in this world.

Under his stepfather's influence, he feels that he has learned more self-control. "He sits back and analyzes things." His mother? "Oh, she will do anything for my brother and me. She spoils us. She wants to give us what she didn't have growing up. She's sensitive. I can't tease her too much."

Joe's goal is to pass his GED (General Educational Development) and then join the reserves.

"Not the army?" I ask.

"In the army, you have to sign up for a certain length of time, like three years. What if I don't like it? I want to test myself in the reserves first. I don't know if I have the courage."

Underlying self-doubt comes to the surface. His dream may not be fulfilled exactly the way he wishes. Or along the way, as Joe's confidence grows, he may see that different options are available. Solving algebra problems, a task he once thought beyond him, has already laid those math demons to rest. One day he will see himself as others see him — a noble, tender-hearted man — and his dream may take a different form. For now, he adores his teacher and is getting what he has always wanted, wise and thoughtful attention and validation every time he walks into the Learning Centre.

Two certainties prevail by the end of our meetings: Joe, the world is a better place because you are in it, and your teacher is right — you are an inspiration.

An Afternoon of Aramaic
CAROL KNEPPER

"You've got to be faking!" the resource teacher exclaimed with no small degree of annoyance. "You did five chapters of that novel just yesterday!"

Jason couldn't make head or tail of the jumble of letters on the page. They might as well have been Aramaic or Mandarin, or perhaps some strange script from one of the Cyrillic languages with their upside-down *n*'s and backward *p*'s. In any case, they didn't mean anything to him, and there was nothing he could do about it.

On the previous day, he really *had* worked through several chapters of the novel during resource time. By the next afternoon, nothing made sense. His teacher's grasp of dyslexia (like that of many in the school system) may have been somewhat tenuous, and she assumed he must be joking around or simply shirking. For him to remain in resource support would be a waste of time, and thus Jason's long-term involvement with the program was terminated. He was in high school by then anyway, the better part of his haphazard education completed. The experience of that teenage moment was branded on his memory.

People with dyslexia have good and bad days. On some occasions, Jason can read relatively well, but the next day or hour or minute, that ability inexplicably vanishes. People who have diabetes experience ups and downs, literally, in terms of blood sugar, and no one accuses them of pretence. Perhaps we have a better grasp of readily observable disorders. Like some physical conditions, dyslexia seems to run in families. Jason has a brother and a cousin with the condition, and they, too, deal with the accompanying challenges.

A frank young man, Jason is quick to respond to my queries. "It makes the words look weird," he tells me, "and it's pretty hard to describe to someone who doesn't have it. I can read individual letters, although as a kid it took me a long time to catch on."

Many people think that people with dyslexia consistently reverse *b*'s and *d*'s or read words backwards, but that is a bit of a stereotype, held even by many teachers. "In dog we trust," so to speak, would be simple, but it is hardly realistic for the many who struggle with this widely varying condition. If things were consistent, those with dyslexia would simply learn that *b* would always look like *d*, *p* like *q*, and make that adaptation. But it is not like that at all, and therein lies the problem. "Nothing is ever the same from one time to the next," Jason explains. "A *b* might look like a *d* sometimes, but it can take many other forms as well. It might look like a number or symbol of some sort, or like nothing I can even recognize."

Jason always had difficulty with reading and repeated grade one as a result. "I probably could have stood to repeat again, but it would not have made a lot of difference," he admits. "It took me until grade three to learn to write my *abc*'s." By that time, Jason had a teaching assistant, as students with dyslexia often do; they commonly need test questions read to them and their responses scribed, assistance with note-taking, and instructions reviewed step-by-step. Not until Jason was ten or eleven did he undergo school-based testing — such delays are not uncommon in an underfunded system. It was then that he received the official diagnosis of dyslexia. "I was a kid, and I figured if that's what they said I had, I had it," he tells me. Children tend to accept what adults say about diagnoses, even if they do not understand the implications.

Jason recalls that his schooling was frustrating. He was pushed through the system with no real achievement in terms of literacy skills. Even more frustrating was his experience of seeing good programs pulled from the school. "I remember having success with one — I think it was called 'Hooked on Phonics' — in grade five. I had worked my way into the second book when it was cut, and I was left out in the cold."

Jason started doing physical labour as early as grade seven, working at one point for Mr. Dumpster, a refuse-collection company. "School wasn't really helping me," he ponders, "and sometimes we would sit in the resource room eating popcorn and watching movies. That's just how it was a lot of the time — a bit of a joke." He describes his entire education as a farce. Each year, with the exception of grade one, he was promoted. "So much of that was bogus," he states in his matter-of-fact manner. "It made me mad in a way to be automatically pushed ahead like that without having learned anything."

In time, like most people with dyslexia, Jason learned to work around his reading challenges. "If I had to read a book and afterwards write a report or essay, I had to use my imagination to follow the book and put something down on paper. I also learned to pick up on what might be asked on a test or exam. I would try to create my own story mentally and then go back to it at test time, using my story to get me through the test questions. I learned to use a creative way of thinking, and having an imagination is not a bad thing."

Jason speaks with candour of his condition, with no resentment or bitterness whatsoever. His positive attitude is living proof of the strength he has found in adversity. By the time he reached the higher grades, he had come to more or less accept his inability to read, just as one accepts one's hair colour or handedness. It was just the way things were, a part of his identity. Just before graduation, he spoke with his principal about his inadequate skills. He claims it felt odd to have nearly finished school and not have mastered the skills required for gainful employment. Jason entered the adult world of work, even though he says he "couldn't read and could barely do math."

Jason has found that dyslexia poses just as much of a hurdle at work as it did at school. "I have held many different jobs, pretty much physical work, and there are always challenges to work around. I am always direct about my reading problem."

Dyslexia is not a condition a person could successfully hide for long, and in his job searches, Jason has found it best to deal in a forthright manner with his particular challenges. An interesting and animated storyteller, he recounts his adventures as a cab driver. "For a while, I drove a cab. Of course, I had no problem with the random pick-ups, but the call-ins — when I had to read street signs to find an address — were difficult. I am nervous in certain situations, such as trying to find a house, but I have no trouble retaining street names and locations once I am familiar with them."

He describes other day-to-day issues with which he copes. "I often reverse telephone numbers and have a hard time reading signs, but I do okay if I actually see the item, like a compressor with a manual. I can't read the instructions, so I operate on common sense. One time, there was a complicated machine with a list of instructions beside it that I needed to be able to follow to get a job. I knew I could never read them, but I could use logic, which told me exactly what those directions must have been. The guy hired me on that basis, and I stayed at that job quite a while."

"The secretaries are usually great," Jason comments. "One went over delivery routes with me before I started out, and that helped a lot. Once they know I have trouble reading, they just say 'no problem' and help me out."

On one of his jobs, Jason had to deliver a load of gravel on his own, and he relates in his easy conversational manner how his inability to read affected him. "I drove all over, trying to find the house, based on the directions and description they gave me. I finally found something that looked like it, with a clearing beside the house, but I wasn't sure I had the right place until a man came outside and told me where to back up. I ended up sticking with this job."

Logic is a word Jason uses a great deal. "Most of the time, I use logic, since I can't rely on written words like other people. One thing about my dyslexia is that it forces me to think, and that isn't bad. I have met really educated people with degrees and stuff who can't think outside the box or beyond the manual."

Even in social settings, such as restaurants, a reading disability has its trials. "I either order the same thing all the time or get whatever someone else is having," he tells me. "I end up with a lot of burgers and hot sandwiches. Menus are hard to decipher, and I know the choices in the places I usually go. Some situations make me nervous, but I manage."

When asked if he ever had given up, he responded readily. "I can honestly say that I have never given up. If I had, I wouldn't be getting up and going out to work every day — I'd be on the street. I have tried different programs. Not too long ago, I got into Read Saint John through the Saint John Learning Exchange. I couldn't do the independent work like you have to at the Learning

Exchange, but I did finally find a tutor through them. I go to tutoring on Tuesday evenings, and the one-on-one helps. I have made some progress, and every little bit counts."

Incentives are important to any worker, and Jason mentions that sometimes a person is penalized when attempting self-improvement in the form of courses or tutoring. "You shouldn't lose a few hours' pay when you need to take time from work to upgrade yourself," he says. "That doesn't make any sense at all."

Jason, upbeat and positive, has recently found great motivation from two daughters, ages eighteen months and three years. "I want to be able to read to them at bedtime. I want to help them with their school work when the time comes. I want to earn a decent living."

Several years ago, in the resource room of his semi-rural school, when the words of that novel appeared as a foreign language, the misconceptions that surround dyslexia first became real to him. Since then, one of Jason's favourite expressions is, "It all comes down to reality." And he has faced reality with admirable fortitude.

Through Allan's Eyes

EVELYN BUTCHER

"I'll be wearing a Senators cap," Allan told me over the phone, as we set up our meeting at Chatham's local public library. And then we were in front of each other, two total strangers each on a mission: he with a story to tell; I with a story to write. Tall and thick through the shoulders and chest, he was dressed in casual clothes with an Ottawa Senators cap pulled down almost to the top of his sunglasses. I asked about his cap, a Christmas gift from his friend Wally. He told me the Senators are his favourite hockey team.

Talk of his cap led to a story. As an athlete in the Special Olympics, his team went to Ottawa in 2000 to compete in curling, and they won a bronze medal. After their win, his team was taken to the Corel Centre (now called Scotiabank Place) to see an NHL game between the Ottawa Senators and the St. Louis Blues. Even though the Senators lost, Allan assured me it was a great experience.

He described himself as cute and loveable, a momma's boy, "and that's okay with me. Mom gave me pretty well everything I wanted. I guess you could say she spoiled me. But my grandmother, she really spoiled me; there was just nothing she wouldn't let me do. When I was a kid, a sleepover at Grammy's house was great. She allowed me to eat lots of junk food — she always had a stash of special treats. She spoiled me rotten. I still enjoy junk food. Lemon meringue pie, there's nothing that tastes as good as homemade pie!"

In contrast, he doesn't hold the same fondness for his memories of school. "Going to school wasn't that great. I didn't like the outdoor stuff very much, especially always having to stay with the special needs people. I guess I was slow in learning to read, so I went to a special needs class. Some of those kids were bullied, so we were kept from mixing with the rest of the kids on the playground. It was supposed to be good for us, but to me it felt like segregation. It didn't seem fair that we couldn't play with the other kids. It was like we weren't equal.

"Always being sent to different schools, not knowing anyone was confusing too. In grade one, I was a half year at one school, a half year at another school, not promoted. Back to the first school again for the second year in grade one. Then to the other again in grade two. Special needs classes were only available in town, so I was bused about twenty-five miles. I didn't know anyone because they were all ahead of me then. I was a stranger again in grade two. I had no guy friends there and had to hang out with girls. Everyone called me 'sissy.' I wasn't held back any more grades there, though.

"I went to junior high school in town. I was held back again in grade nine. I had the marks, but my teacher said I wasn't ready for high school. In class, it seemed I was always the one raising my hand and asking for help. As soon as a teacher gave us an assignment I would try to do it, then I'd have to raise my hand. Yeah, it was like, 'Hey teacher, I need some help here.' It was embarrassing sometimes, because when I raised my hand and asked for help some of the other kids would giggle. I always needed help with written instructions in reading and math.

"When I finally did get to high school, my teachers were great. I remember one especially; he was the greatest. He told me he could teach me to be a good man. I never forgot that, and I am a good man. I was picked on a lot all through school — bullying, name-calling, and playing tricks on me. In high school, a group of boys who hung out together would block the corridor and refuse to let me pass to go to class. They would make me walk all around the school to get to my class. They would snicker as I entered class late every day. They knew why I was late, but nobody ever told. I was always given homework but managed to get it done at school. I had to do an extra year in grade twelve, and then I graduated."

It has been seventeen years since high school graduation. What are Allan's goals now? "I still dream of going to college so I can learn more. I like to see people learn, and I really want to earn my BA. When I graduated, I wanted to go to college, but I was told by the high school counsellor that I couldn't go for a BA but maybe a trade school like NBCC. I sent applications to three different colleges and was accepted by one. When I saw what it cost for four years — over forty thousand dollars — I just went *'whew.'* I didn't have that kind of money. I wouldn't ask Mom for help, so I guess I kind of had to give up. I graduated years ago, but I still want to go to college.

"A person I know quite well and who knew I had trouble with reading and math told me about a program available to help adults improve their literacy skills. She told me about the Laubach Literacy course. I asked about it. When I was accepted I just went, 'Cool!' I was so glad to get started. My tutor is great. Yeah, I like her. She has a full-time job and volunteers with Laubach Literacy, so if her work schedule changes, we have to meet at different times. Mostly we try to meet once a week. I've been with this tutor for about a year. Some of it was hard, learning all the letter sounds. I'm about half finished. In about a year, I should be finished my course. Then, I just hope college will be next. Completing the Laubach Literacy course will help me to understand material better in reading and math, so I will be better prepared for college. Lately, I'm thinking about becoming a coach or trainer in physical fitness."

Until then, Allan is building a life for himself. "I share an apartment with some friends now, and do all my own cooking and housework. Sometimes when I make pasta, I cook enough for us all, but mostly I just cook for myself. Living with some friends is a good arrangement right now."

Allan keeps very busy, employed every summer for the past decade at NBCC Miramichi. He does volunteer work in his spare time. He frequently works evenings and weekends doing janitorial work. He gets along well with his colleagues and considers them extended family. Allan likes to hang out with friends and his work buddies. Together they jokingly refer to themselves as the "Trailer Park Boys."

Allan shows me some the medals he has received for competing in various sports, an impressive assortment of about forty gold, silver, and bronze. He has also been awarded numerous mementos and many honorary gifts for his volunteer services around the city. He volunteers with Phantoms Senior C hockey team, midget baseball, and wheelchair sports. He also works with the Special Olympics teams.

"In 2003, I was on the Special Olympics softball team and went to Surrey, British Columbia, to compete. We won a silver medal. The Canada Games were going on at the same time, and we were allowed to watch lots of Canadian competitions. It was a great trip. We lost luggage, changed planes twice, and experienced jet lag. I was really tired out when I landed back home. I missed work the next day. With Special Olympics soccer in 2005, we played in Saskatchewan and won a bronze medal that year. We'll be competing in Fredericton for the 2009 nationals in curling.

"One of my best summer adventures last year was going to Moncton as volunteer equipment manager with the midget baseball team. I saw them win the provincial championship. Each team member received a medal. I was awarded a medal with 2008 Champions on it. They announced my name, referring to me as a 'number one fan.' I also received a token jersey for my contributions to the team. The midget win entitles the team to compete in the national championships in Fredericton. I'm going on that trip with them. I might be the first one there."

We took a day to explore Allan's old neighbourhood. I thought an outing would help us to feel more comfortable and to talk candidly. As we drove along the winding country roads, Allan pointed out numerous special spots along the river. With enthusiasm he showed me the old fish hatchery, where his dad took him many times to watch the fish. When we passed the abandoned schoolyard, he pointed to a big tree that he and his grade one friends enjoyed climbing. Allan remembered falling from it once and cutting his knee. As we crossed the Somers Bridge, he recalled the delightful thrill of jumping off the bridge in summer to cool off.

In spite of the difficult experiences at school, his quiet confidence has helped Allan forge a wide circle of friends and acquaintances with his volunteer and sports involvement. Through Allan's eyes, his present goal of achieving literacy is a stepping stone toward his dream of attending college. His enthusiasm for life and learning spur him on his way.

Letting Her Own Light Shine
LAURA WELLS

"My daughter . . . before she goes to bed, she says, 'Mom, you read so good.' And that makes me feel good."

The desire to be able to read to her children prompted Elaine, a petite, gracious mother of three, to return to school. She compared her first day in 2007 at the Independent Living Centre in Chatham to a child's first day of school. "I was nervous. I had butterflies. It's scary. But I wanted to do it," she says. "I thought that maybe later on in life I'll read to my [younger] children, and get a good job. And it makes you feel good."

Some of Elaine's anxiety and hesitation about learning stem from the poor experiences she has had in the school system. Elaine completed high school. She graduated at the age of eighteen, but she did not enjoy school because it was not always a nice place. She feels that the education system failed her. "All they wanted to do was push you through school and get you out as fast as they can," Elaine says, "and that's what they did to me . . . they shouldn't have done what they did. They should have given me more time to work on my work, and if they wouldn't have pushed me through school, I probably would have had a good job by now." She remembers being hurried along whether or not she understood, always forced onto the next topic in the curriculum. She regrets her school experiences and the impact they have had on her life.

Elaine appreciates her present learning environment at the Independent Living Centre. She does not feel rushed by her tutor as she did by her high-school teachers. "This is what I like, one-on-one. I'd rather not be in a class at all. I know I'd feel really nervous and shy. He [Elaine's tutor] already asked me 'Would you like to go to college?' I said 'Not right now' because I'd feel like I'm nothing 'cause these other students probably would be a lot smarter than I am. And I don't want to feel like I'm nothing." Through her glasses Elaine's brown eyes gaze penetratingly at me.

She talks about the kinds of jobs she had hoped for when she was younger. "My biggest goal of all was working in a restaurant or being a school teacher, but right now a huge goal is to get myself through my books. I'll see how fast I learn and then if my money and my math are good, then I'll see what my tutor thinks."

Elaine is unsure of her abilities and seeks reassurance and guidance from her tutor. "I like him," she tells me. "He's very kind, very gentle. And he'll listen. If I have problems, he's there to help me through." She jokes that although Cyril used to be a principal, he isn't strict. "He's pretty easygoing." He has been Elaine's tutor since she began adult education in 2007. The pair normally meet once a week, on Tuesday mornings at the Independent Living Centre. What is meant to be an hour session typically turns into an hour and a half; about half the time is devoted to studying math and the remaining time is for reading. Cyril is helping Elaine to improve her skills in addition, subtraction, multiplication, and division. She is also learning about money, how to count it, how to add and subtract it, and how to make change. He tries to meet her needs and interests by providing her with reading materials she will enjoy and encouraging her interest in cooking. He has even shared some of his own recipes with her — 'Cyril's Skor Bars' for example. "He's very understanding and he has helped me a long way. I encourage any adult if you need help, don't be shy. Go and ask. There is help there."

She shows me the books she has been working on. She acknowledges difficulty with spelling but says she would really like to be able to spell on her own someday. She expresses how good she feels when she is able to do the work on her own. Cyril sometimes gives her a mix of materials as a challenge. "Some of this is about a grade nine [level]," she says, "and he was quite surprised that I could do this. He said, 'You did it! I'm proud of you.'"

Elaine lights up when she talks about her three children: Daniel (nineteen), Bradley (nine), and Angela (six). "My oldest, he's in college." Daniel is taking a two-year course in youth care at the nearby New Brunswick Community

College in Chatham. "He's struggling with it," Elaine says. "He doesn't know whether to keep on." She knows first-hand about struggles with education. She is hopeful that her son will continue and successfully complete his course.

Her daughter often comes home from school and starts reading, "I say 'Go read. Go do it.'" She agrees that having her daughter see her reading makes her keen to imitate her mother. "What I would want to say to any adult who has problems reading or they're scared to go back to school is that person should do it, because how are our children going to learn to read if we don't go and do it?"

Elaine talks about her hobbies. She tells me that she, her husband, and their oldest son play in a darts league. Elaine enjoys the game but is anxious about tallying the points. She worries she will make a mistake or be too slow, so she gets Daniel to count for her. She loves to cook. "I can read a recipe. If I have problems with the words in a recipe, my husband will help me. He can help me with it." She also likes to crochet and spend time with friends. We come back to the subject of reading, a more recent hobby. When Elaine is not reading her homework assignments, she likes to read romance novels. "There's sometimes words I have a hard time reading," she admits, "but I try and find them out, and now I've got a Bible. I'll sit down and I'll read. When I go to church on Sunday, I'll bring it."

Adult learning has given Elaine a feeling of empowerment and a sense of accomplishment. She is more able to help her children with their homework, she is feeling hopeful about the future, and she has been encouraged to chase her own dreams. What are some of those dreams? For now, she wants to continue improving her reading and math abilities. In the future, her goal is to tackle spelling. Writing will happen later, she informs me. "I already know how to write, but it wouldn't hurt [to learn more]. I love it." In the long-term, Elaine would like to work towards getting a part-time job, which is why math skills are especially important to her. Money is a difficult concept for her, and she feels that she would have difficulty working with her present math skills. She mentions that she would also enjoy working as a caregiver for the elderly, "Just helping elderly women, helping around the house."

In her book *Return to Love*, Marianne Williamson writes: "We were born to make manifest the glory . . . that is within us. It is not just in some of us; it is in everyone. As we let our own light shine, we unconsciously give other people permission to do the same. As we are liberated from our own fear, our presence automatically liberates others."[†] Elaine is a quietly courageous woman who lives the truth of this statement every day.

[†]   Marianne Williamson, *Return to Love: Reflections on the Principles of a 'Course in Miracles'*. (New York: HarperCollins, 1992), chapter 7, section 3.

James's Attitude Makes the Difference
JUNE HORSMAN

According to writer Charles Swindoll, "Attitude, to me, is more important than facts. It is more important than the past, than education, than money, than circumstances, than failures, than successes, than what people think or say or do. It is more important than appearances, giftedness, or skill."[‡] James showed me how the right attitude will take a person places and allow him to do things that he never would have attempted had he looked at just the facts. James is a happy, confident man, despite years of frustration as he struggled through a poorly structured education system. He is proof that a positive attitude can help to compensate for lost opportunities and provide the tools for a brighter future.

James, one of eight children, grew up in Dieppe, New Brunswick, and began grade one in an English school that no longer exists. He went through grades one, two, and three and then started all over again. James explained that he was moved along, and when it was apparent that he could not keep up with the class, it was suggested that he begin over again.

James could not learn to read by the method used to instruct the other students. At that time there was a school in Moncton offering "special education" programs to those who had trouble coping in a "regular" class. James was bused to this school. He recalled some of the other students and the good memories of those days. He enjoyed the woodworking shop and was quick to pick up some of the carpentry skills that proved useful later in his life. This school was geared to teach skills and to address children at their

---

[‡]   This quote taken from wikipedia.org, at http://home.xnet.com/~ansible/attitude.html, accessed May 2009.

individual level, recognizing that not everyone learns at the same pace or in the same manner. The school closed when children with learning challenges were integrated into the public school system. New methods to evaluate and teach were part of this new approach, but they were too late to be of any use to James.

He knew early on that he would have to depend on his memory and listening skills to master things. Difficulty with the printed word meant that he would have to find a way to learn by listening and remembering. His optimistic attitude helped him cope with new challenges, such as having to attend a school away from his neighbourhood, a different school from the one his siblings attended. James was much too busy doing what was necessary to have time for self-pity. Even as a lad he was resourceful. He remembered picking blueberries and selling a whole crate for $7.35 to a canteen located on the marsh and referred to by the locals as "Hard Times Gallant."

After James completed his schooling and graduated into the world at sixteen, he went to work as a roofer. He was a dedicated employee, but this job was seasonal; James wanted full-time employment. He landed a position at a large tire warehouse. He paid attention to details and was able to identify the different types of tires and the many makes and sizes. His struggles with reading had compelled him to be clever in other ways to compensate.

When I asked him if he had ever been hassled at work, he recalled one incident where a foreman was critical of a minor mistake. The foreman reported the mistake to the boss and requested they meet in the office. James acknowledged his error and told the two men, "I can stay here and listen to your story, but I should go back to work and not waste time here." James continued to work at the tire warehouse for the next twenty years.

When the business was sold to another company, James, by then in his forties, was out of a job. He was referred to NBCC by Manpower (now Service Canada). In those days, when people were out of work they registered with this government department. If the agency could not find employment for their clients, then they encouraged upgrading. Today, NBCC has a full-time literacy coordinator who assesses adults and directs them into an appropriate program. Regional Learning Councils find tutors for those not quite ready to receive instruction in a group. This service offers adult learners a chance to get their GED.

The Laubach tutoring James was offered proved to be a turning point. Even though upgrading his reading and math skills would demand time and hard work, he decided "to take a chance." His wife, Evelyn, and his children supported his effort. Evelyn, in fact, was his number one cheerleader.

James began his adult learning with Ed. Through patient one-on-one teaching, Ed helped James begin a journey that soon improved his literacy level. Louise was another tutor who helped James gain confidence and knowledge. Through training and experience he was able to read, write, and communicate much better.

Most of us are timid about public speaking, but James began to speak to school children and other groups. He reminded his audiences to keep going and not give up. He described his personal journey of learning to read as an adult, a process that took years with help from his tutors. Later, he started speaking on behalf of other adult learners. James was an original member of the Student Support group connected with LLNB, and he eventually became co-chair. He gave strong leadership and brought fresh ideas to help new adult learners.

In 1999, James attended a conference in Ottawa as a representative and member of the New Brunswick Student Advisory Committee. In the same year, he received the Award of Merit from Governor General Roméo LeBlanc, who made the presentation in Ottawa at a conference for Laubach Literacy of Canada. In 2001, James was selected as student of the year, earning the Alpha Award for Learner Achievement. He attended provincial, regional, and national conferences as a student and member of LLNB.

"There are many takers," James says. "I believe in giving back." Part of the giving back is to his family. He is proud of his wife and four children. Their youngest son is now in university. James's face lights up when he speaks of his four grandchildren and his joy in being able to read to them. He also took his elderly father to what would be his last Remembrance Day service, despite many obstacles and folks telling him it could not be done. James overcame opposition from other people and found a way to take his infirm father to this public event. It was a very meaningful experience for both of them. James felt good about honouring his father's wishes to be at the ceremony. Once again, his "can" attitude carried him over hurdles to achieve what he set out to do.

James has a keen interest in his community. He mentions that he would like to capture his mother's stories on tape and record some of the oral history from that generation. He also takes pride in his job at a local golf club. He volunteers when there is a need. He drives a van for his church, having received his chauffeur's licence.

James's spirit and remarkable attitude have stood him in good stead for meeting the many obstacles along his journey to achieving literacy. His stance is firm on never giving up. What would he tell others struggling with illiteracy? "Don't be scared; I've been there. Take a chance."

I Wanted to Better Myself

RICHARD TOTH

Maurice was twenty-eight years old when he contacted Laubach Literacy in 1978. He was married, and he had two young sons. In my several conversations with him, the question I kept returning to was, "What did you expect to gain when you first contacted Laubach Literacy?" At first Maurice said that he simply wanted to "better himself." His answer intrigued me, and I wanted to find out more. Maurice has the look of a man who can solve problems. He is trim and muscular, and he has a working man's hands. His answers are to the point. He is not comfortable with small talk.

We met in Maurice's Tim Horton's franchise, one of a string of businesses he owns, on a very busy corner in east Bathurst. As well as housing Tim Horton's, the main building includes a convenience store and a bakery outlet. Outside there is a six-pump gas bar. Behind the main building there is a separate structure that houses the office of Maurice's trailer rental business as well as a car wash stall and a garage. The garage is for servicing the line of gasoline and diesel tractors that he imports from China. They stood out, and I had to ask about them.

"I usually go to China once a year," he said. "I go right to their factories and buy direct. They sell for a lot less than those made in North America."

"What made you decide to sell them?"

"Well, we spend part of the winter in Florida. There was a guy selling them there. In the United States they are sold under a different name. He was selling a tractor down there for seven thousand dollars. One the same size made here would sell for twice as much, or more. The guy in Florida was making a good profit. So I contacted the factory in China and went over there to look. I pay for bringing them in myself, but I'm able to sell them for less than those made here."

"Are they as good?"

"There's no difference when it comes to the engine or the drive train. What's different is that the Chinese tractors are good, basic tractors. Not everyone needs the fancy stuff. I sold sixty of them last year."

The corner that Maurice owns hummed with activity while we talked. Behind the main building there is a line of used cars and trucks for sale. Maurice also imports used travel trailers and all-terrain vehicles from the United States. On the other side of Bathurst, in the town of Beresford, Maurice owns a strip mall that includes another convenience store and gas bar. Space there is rented to a large fitness centre, a hairdresser, a tanning centre, a laundromat, and a paintball supply store. Maurice mentioned that he has other properties and business interests.

When Maurice said that he contacted Laubach Literacy because he wanted to better himself, he did not mean financially. He achieved financial success at a relatively young age due to his businessman's view of the world and an entrepreneurial spirit. He has always been a hard worker; his family set the example. "My parents had eleven children," he said, "seven boys and four girls. Not everyone went through school but everyone worked."

In fact, formal schooling was sporadic. "We lived quite a ways out of town. The buses didn't always run. I did go through the grades up to high school, but not much of it stuck with me. I couldn't remember all the little things about reading and writing. I just wasn't that interested. You remember what you are interested in."

When he was fifteen, in 1965, he started working at the Kent store in Bathurst. It was the largest general merchandiser in the city. At the same time, Maurice's older brother Leonard was working as an industrial painter in Ontario. Maurice saw that he would be able to do better as a painter than he would if he continued stocking shelves, so he left to join his brother. At George Brown College in Toronto, he took the apprenticeship training program and earned his certificate as a licensed painter. When Leonard decided to return to Bathurst and start his own paint contracting company, Maurice returned with him. Together the two brothers started Maritime Steeplejack Limited. The business prospered and the company grew.

"How many people did you employ when Maritime Steeplejack was at its peak?"

"Around seventy-five. We did all kinds of jobs, from painting to construction to demolition. One of the first contracts was to paint windows and window frames for one of the schools here in the city. Afterwards, we did buildings and bridges. We had a contract at the lead-zinc smelter in Belledune from 1973 until 1985. There was a lot of work at Brunswick Mines. We did jobs all over. We had a contract with the CNR for five years."

Maurice sold his shares of Maritime Steeplejack to his brother in 1985. He employs about forty people altogether in the business he runs now.

When Maurice approached Laubach more than three decades ago, he could read some things, but he wanted to be able to read better. He wanted to be able to read all of the bedtime stories that his boys asked for. Writing posed the biggest challenge for him.

"You could write a letter, for example?"

"I can write a letter for me, but not for you," he answered with an appraising look. "It's all the little things. They don't stick in my head. As I said, you remember what you are interested in. In school I wasn't all that interested."

"How long did you continue with tutoring?"

"I don't exactly remember how long, every week for maybe a year or two. I went long enough to realize that it would take me as many years as I had gone to school to get all the little things, spelling, how words go together — grammar. It was hard being tutored," he added. "I don't have a memory for little things."

He told me about a contract he had accepted to dismantle a large structure and its components at a pulp mill in the United States. It was a complicated and time-consuming job that required care because the dismantled equipment would be hauled to a different location and then reassembled. When the job was completed, he was asked to submit a report on what the job had entailed. He wrote the report, but since then he has always felt that it reflected poorly on him.

"I shouldn't have written that report. Or I should have told someone else what the job was and they could have written it, and then it would have been written up correctly. That's what I do now. But I've always felt badly about that report. Even now when I need to write an important letter, one of my secretaries writes down what I want to say, and they put it in the right language.

"Writing a good report is always important. Being able to read other reports is important. You can do a job and you can do it really well. Maybe someone else who wouldn't even know how to start the job writes the report. And they can get the credit for it, as if they had done the work themselves."

"The time that you spent being tutored, did it help?"

"It helped some. I didn't stick with it long enough. It wasn't a waste of time, no. I did do it, and that was important, too."

"Finance and business has never been a problem for you, Maurice."

"No, math I've always had. And when it comes to running a business, well, you don't do that by yourself. If you have good people around you, they make it work. You do have to know what you are doing. I know a lot of people who know about things that I don't. When it comes to complicated contracts and agreements, well, my lawyer tells me what I need to know. It's okay now. My son will own most of this business in a few more years," he added. "I'm selling my shares to him over time. Both of my sons went to university." Maurice's sons have learned everything they need to know to carry on the business.

"Is there anything else you wanted to do back then that you thought tutoring might help you to do?"

"I was thinking about going into politics back then. If I was going to do that I would have to know how to write a good report, and I would need to be able to read all kinds of reports."

I looked around at the obvious success he had achieved with his existing skills and know-how. "Maybe you should reconsider going into politics, Maurice. We need people who know how to make things work."

He offered a guarded smile. "I don't really think so, but you never know."

Life Is Amazing
JUDY BOWMAN

During her third month of therapy, Patricia, in her late forties, spent the hour studying the way her fingers knitted and tangled in her lap. She hadn't spoken other than to say that she called herself Pat. The colour of her eyes was a mystery because she couldn't make eye contact. One day, by accident or by opportunity, her head lifted, revealing the dull glaze of defeat in her hazel eyes. In her fourth month of therapy, Pat still didn't speak but something happened. She cried — not the rending sobbing you would expect knowing that she had survived an abusive marriage and was finally free — but a steady trickle of tears that captured the light as they marked a path down her pale thin cheeks, cheeks that had been slapped and punched and shoved into walls and floors.

About six years thereafter, a wide smile warms Pat's face, her eyes sparkle behind her glasses. She waves a paycheque in her hands. "Look!" She points to the stub. Her tallied hours reach one hundred.

Since 2003, Pat's life has changed dramatically. She has been restoring her life, her beliefs about her intelligence and abilities, and most importantly, her limitations. She has questioned and rejected her entire self-image regarding her education. Eager to share her story, she believes it will help others overcome their own difficulties.

"My heart goes out to women I see in my position. I was ready to go, and I *could* go, knowing my husband was in jail and couldn't reach me and convince me to stay. I finally woke up. I sat in my therapist's office and couldn't open my mouth, but once the tears started, everything began to wash away. The heavy burden on me was lifted. It was an amazing feeling. I've been down there, and now, I'm up here." Her hands mark the wide difference. "Anyone can do this."

"At first my family didn't believe that I was serious about leaving. They took me to Mental Health for help, and I needed it, but they thought I should be in a group home where others could look after me.

"I got really upset. I said a few things they didn't want to hear. Some of my family accepted it, some didn't. They didn't think I had it in me to look after myself. I think it was because I was the baby of the family, and they had their own ideas of what I was able to do. They had watched me struggle for years in my marriage, unable to help myself. Plus, they always bossed me around. But I told them I was capable of doing so. Though I didn't know how I was going to do it, I was determined to better myself."

Soon after becoming independent, Pat suffered a stroke. "The doctors said it was from all the stress and the abuse I went through. My father died in March 2003. My sister passed away in March 2004. It all hit me at once, but I was fortunate." Apart from a blocked blood vessel in her neck, which was not treated, Pat did not suffer any physical or mental deficit from the stroke. Following her recovery, the process of beginning to better herself began. Pat's therapist had pre-registered her with New Directions Community Academic Services for the Community Adult Learning Program (CALP) at Lobban House. She was confident that Pat could improve her literacy skills.

"The coordinator of the program believed in me," she recalls. Through this program, Pat discovered she wasn't "stupid" — a trait that her own siblings had reinforced in her since she was a preschooler, and later her husband had followed suit.

Having support and encouragement from her instructors was a new experience for Pat. Her ideas about her intelligence and abilities had been shaped by her family and others in her community. She can't identify one specific reason for their assessment.

"They thought I was slow learning. I don't know whether it was because we were poor or that I was lower class or just different from them. But the kids at school made fun of me. They used to tease me about my clothes. Mom used to make long johns out of flour bags for us to wear to keep us warm on the walk to school. We walked a mile to and from school. No buses."

Pat's parents did not complete their education. "Dad had only grade six, but he could read and write. Mom could read and write, but I don't know what grade she went to. Back then, my father had a choice: go to school or go in the woods. He chose the woods to survive. With ten girls and two boys, he didn't have much choice."

Attending school reinforced Pat's distorted belief in her learning abilities. "The teachers thought I was one of those kids that didn't know anything and that I wouldn't make anything of my life. So I thought, maybe I am stupid, maybe I can't do this."

Pat describes herself as stubborn and determined. These qualities have served her well. Against all odds, she graduated with a grade twelve diploma at the age of twenty-one. "The teachers knew it was all up to me. I tried the best I could, and they saw that. I didn't have any special help at that time because they didn't know about learning disabilities."

Pat recalls that her mother and father had faith in her. Her mother passed away before she graduated. The Christmas after she died, Pat's father gave her a charm bracelet from her mother, a family heirloom. "My father told me my mother always knew I was going to graduate and had this put away for the occasion."

At CALP, Pat began to understand her literacy issues and to receive the necessary assistance. "I had different needs while learning. Before, I just thought I couldn't. My reading and writing skills weren't very good. I was below average. My other marks were fine and my spelling was exceptional.

"When one of the teachers at CALP told me there were no stupid questions, I began to ask for help. I always thought my reading was okay because I could say the words, but I couldn't comprehend it. People used to say I should understand what was required, but I didn't even understand the questions. I found when a passage was read back to me, I could understand the content. I learned I could read but not comprehend."

Memorizing is a honed skill for her. "I got through school by memorizing the lessons, first two lines, then three. I was fine on tests if I wrote down the right lines."

Through different workplace programs, Pat gained work experience, yet she could not imagine getting a job on her own initiative. Last fall, she called a special care home to see if she could drop off a resumé.

"I introduced myself, and after my boss read it, she asked if I could start on Friday. I just stood there. I didn't know what to do. I thought, Is this for real? Was I hearing things?" Pat accepted the job.

She loves her work and her employer understands her reading challenges. "My employer is very helpful. She took me under her wing when I started and knows how to suggest different ways of helping me grasp ideas. She would read labels and directions to me and I would read them to her and then we would compare our ideas. She taught me about blood sugar, insulin, and other things so I can cope with what I need to do. It is amazing to me that I can do all these things."

Her reading skills improved so that she could assist in an emergency at her place of employment. "I was called and asked to go down to the med room and look in a blue box for one particular med and tell them the number of milligrams on the label. I was able to read and understand the label. And I got it right."

She merely laughs when she thinks that she is working in the same type of special care home her siblings had planned for her.

There is little about her life that Pat doesn't enjoy. Budgeting, saving for new furniture by working extra hours, these are things she thrives on. Though reading and comprehension remain a challenge, she now has a love for learning. Reading will never be a recreational activity, though she thinks she would enjoy books on tape. "I know I should read more, but I read only when I have to. I do love word puzzles, and I can finish a book in an evening."

Pat also has a male friend in her life. Deciding to protect herself before becoming involved in a relationship, she put the lessons learned in therapy to good use. "I was following a pattern with the abuse and I recognized it, so I am very careful about myself. My friend doesn't drink or boss me around. I do what I want to do."

Recently, she met her ex-husband in a store. "At first I was afraid, and then I just walked by him. He used to call me stupid, a moron, and an idiot. I don't believe that now."

Working in a special care home is not her final goal. She plans to train as a Personal Support Worker next fall. As a PSW, Pat will qualify to work in a nursing home or in a hospital. "Every day I work on improving myself. There are a lot of people who believe in me, and I learned that I can do anything I set my mind to. My life is amazing."

Seeing the Bigger Picture

NOELINE BRIDGE

Dennis is a busy man. When I managed to reach him, he assumed I was a member of the press. The media had interviewed him several times. We made our rendezvous at the Irving Big Stop in Salisbury, halfway between Moncton (where I live) and Petitcodiac (where he lives). He had spoken at the GED graduation ceremony in Fredericton the night before.

Dennis grew up in Quispamsis as the fifth child in a family of eight. His father was a supervisor for Atlantic Wholesalers, travelling a lot until heart problems led to his retirement from the road. The family then moved to Petitcodiac, and he ran a grocery store in Salisbury. At that time, Dennis was twenty years old, and he remained in Saint John, where he was working.

Dennis had left school when he finished grade ten, despite his parents' encouragement for their children to stay in school and get a good education. He had no particular problems with learning, but school had never interested him. He got a job with the Crane McAvity machine shop in Saint John. "In those days," he told me, "you could get a job right away with grade ten — heck, you could get a job with no education at all! Now, no one will even look at you unless you have grade twelve."

Dennis has always worked. With a father in full-time employment, his family was "comfortable enough, but money was short for a family with eight kids," so when he was still in school he delivered newspapers and milk and put in a stint at a poultry farm. He caddied at the golf course, lining up very early each morning to make sure he was picked. He explained to me that where he lived, he went to school for only half a day; there were too many pupils for the school facilities, so they went to school in shifts. "As you were getting on the bus to go home at midday, the bus with the kids for the afternoon shift was unloading."

He stayed at Crane McAvity for two years and then ran a convenience store in Saint John for two years. After that, he joined Sobeys, where he trained to become a grocery manager, remaining in the job for five years.

He decided to move to Petitcodiac, to join the rest of his family and look for a local, full-time job. "I didn't intend to stay in Petitcodiac, but I've lived there ever since!" He got a job at Canada Packers, which lasted eleven years. He hit a roadblock when Canada Packers closed, and he was out of work. It was then the late 1980s and times had changed, so he found himself unable to get another job with his grade-ten education. Just to make a living, he worked in the woods, sawing and cutting wood, working six to seven days a week in all weather.

After five years in the woods, he secured a part-time job at Fawcett Lumber in Petitcodiac, working on clean-up and cleaning machinery. When Fawcett Lumber gave him more work, it meant working shifts lasting from 4:30 a.m. to 2:30 p.m. and seventeen hours on Fridays so he could include overtime in his wages. He became the union representative and the co-chair of the health and safety issues committee. He took courses on union matters.

The company advertised frequently for millwrights. Dennis would see the advertisements and want to become a millwright, but grade twelve was required. His wife, Karen, who works as a teacher's assistant, encouraged him to take correspondence courses to build up his education, but he felt he wouldn't be able to manage this while he worked such long hours.

Late in 2007, he received a shock when the Fawcett mill shut down. Over one hundred personnel were laid off in the first round, with another twenty to thirty in the final round. The company brought in counsellors to assist the laid-off workers with their future options. The workers were advised to attend courses at NBCC in Moncton. They would be paid fifteen cents per kilometre for their travel.

They protested: couldn't they go to the Salisbury Adult Learning Centre, which was much nearer their homes? The problem, they were told, was that although the town of Salisbury would pay the rent, heating the centre wasn't paid for by either the town or the government, and they would be taking their courses over the winter. The workers rationalized that by attending the Salisbury Centre instead of going to Moncton, the government would be able to halve the mileage cost, and so couldn't the savings go to the centre for heating? They discovered government financing didn't work that way.

However, the workers were told that if they could find a way to heat the Salisbury Centre, they could study there. They contacted their one local teacher, and her positive attitude convinced them that they wanted to learn from her; she, in her turn, wanted to teach them. So all of them — Dennis, his fellow students, and the teacher — launched a local fundraising campaign for heat, which raised $2,025 and covered the bill.

Dennis found part-time work at a grocery store in Petitcodiac as he began his GED course in the Salisbury Adult Learning Centre at the beginning of November 2007. He passed in May 2008 in all subjects but mathematics. When I remarked that he had made great progress in passing nearly all subjects in only six months, Dennis credited his teacher.

"We had a phenomenal teacher. She made it so interesting that I looked forward to going there every day. It was so unlike school. You could ask her anything — even phone her at home. In her class, no one was smarter than anyone else. If you had an answer, you shared it with all the others."

While he was completing his GED, he took the Speaking Out by Utilizing Learners course from the Literacy Coalition of New Brunswick. He enjoyed this. "Everyone's stories are so different, so interesting." The course led to his public speaking engagements. He explained his speaking style. "One time I made notes and then realized I'd missed a point and didn't know where I was! So I decided not to do that again. I may say one thing one time and not at another. It's different each time."

He plans to retake mathematics at a suitable time in the near future. I asked Dennis what sort of work he wanted to do with his GED.

"Something with the public, [with] young adults and kids." He told me how much he enjoys meeting customers in the grocery store, getting to know them and helping them with their needs. How did he feel he could be a role model for youth? "Share my employment experience — help them to stay in school," he replied. "Our parents always told us that, but we didn't believe them." In turn, he is encouraging his own son, Samuel, to get a good education. "I don't want him to go through the same rough times I did. He's a lot like me. We both like being outdoors, playing hockey, hunting, and fishing." Dennis understands that when your employment shuts down, the more you have to offer, the more you have to fall back on. He pointed out that forestry in New Brunswick is declining — so opportunities in the woods are fewer — and the fisheries are in trouble. "I've learned not to rely on anyone else, that nothing is guaranteed."

Dennis is still involved with union affairs. "It's very rewarding, especially when a person receives rights they're entitled to. Often they don't know what those rights are and need to be told." Fawcett's closing, along with other closures, meant the end of medical coverage, pensions, and life insurance, on which the workers had often relied. He's passionate on the subject of the rights of the marginalized. "I'm very bothered by teasing — bullying — the inequality of women. Karen works, and I share the household work with her." Typical of his busy life, after our meeting at the Salisbury Big Stop, he was off to Montreal the next day for the biennial convention of the Communications, Energy, and Paperworkers (CEP) Union.

Recently, Dennis accepted an invitation to join the board of directors of the Literacy Coalition. "The Literacy Coalition has been excellent to me. They act like a go-between person for us; they're there to help us." He is looking forward to discovering what his role will be on the board. He had taken the Coalition's SOUL course because he felt he had something to give back. He approaches his upcoming responsibilities on the board in the same spirit. "I want to make it easy for learners to have opportunities to develop their literacy skills."

Reading for Love
KATHIE GOGGIN

A loving family, working together, can transform lives. When I first met Bev, his genuine smile and unassuming pride in his accomplishments made an impression. He always had a joke or a funny story ready to lighten the conversation. He put me at ease immediately, and he wanted to talk — not so much about learning to read as an adult as about the importance of family in his life.

Bev is forty-seven years old, the only child of parents who did their best to raise him. His mother stayed at home and took care of the household, while his father worked as a truck driver. It was a typical family except for one thing. Bev explains, "We had TV and radio at home, but no books, newspapers, or magazines." Bev has no recollection of ever having been read to as a young child. There were no bedtime stories when he was tucked in at night because neither of his parents could read. "Mom and Dad were able to read a few basic words, and they could sign their names, but that was all," he says.

It is not surprising then, that when Bev went to school, he struggled with reading. The written word was a new experience for him, and while it had the potential to open up new worlds, reading became more and more difficult as time went on. He was "able to get by picking some things out" when reading, and by writing "the best I could." Bev knew instinctively that he needed more help in those early years, but because none was available at home, the difficulty increased, and he fell further and further behind his classmates. Bev was passed from grade to grade, never having caught up with his peers, and somehow his teachers didn't address his struggles.

"I needed more help. You are in school to learn, and I was in small classes in a rural school. They knew I had problems, but no one gave me extra help." Bev states this matter-of-factly. I am surprised that there is no trace of anger. "It's just how things were back then," he says, shrugging his shoulders and smiling.

Finally, in grade nine, he was put in a special class. "Did you get in trouble back then?" I ask, knowing that children who fall behind in school sometimes act out in their desperation to receive the attention they need.

"No, I never did," he says with an impish grin, "except, for the one time I got caught smoking." And while I can't imagine this amicable person ever having been "a squeaky wheel," demanding the much deserved extra help he required, listening to his story, I share the frustration he must have felt.

When I ask him about his life now, there is a sense of contentment. He is happy to work, spend time with his family, and travel the old railway bed on his four-wheeler. Life is full.

Bev met his wife, Krista, eighteen years ago, at a bowling match. When I meet with his family, I notice caring glances and smiles still pass easily between them, especially when talking about the mutual pride they share in their two sons. Times are a bit easier now, but they weren't always this good. When they first married, Bev was managing two jobs at once, working extra-long hours to make ends meet. At the time, he hoped to get hired on with the school district — a higher-paying, more secure job with better benefits and hours. But when Bev went to apply, he discovered that he needed to pass a written examination in order to be a custodian.

Even though he had the qualifications and experience, "I didn't get the job because I couldn't read and that meant I couldn't write the test," he says without a trace of bitterness. Rather than becoming discouraged and giving up, at the urging of his wife, he contacted Laubach Literacy. Krista was already interested in literacy and had attended Laubach sessions to learn how to teach reading, but she didn't want to teach her own husband.

"That doesn't always work so well," she says with a laugh and a knowing look.

Bev says Krista told him in no uncertain terms, "You are going to Laubach. So I went."

Going to Laubach wasn't easy. It was a huge step, and Bev was very nervous about it. "I wouldn't have gone if it wasn't for my wife," he says, making clear the importance of Krista's influence in his life. Bev has learned how to read, even after having to recover from a heart attack just two weeks into the reading program.

Eventually, he did go back to take the test for the custodial job but didn't get it. Instead, he was hired part time. He persisted and has since worked his way into the better job as a school custodian that he had set his sights on. He states this with obvious pride and some relief. "Now I work days, 6:30 a.m. to 3:00 p.m., five days per week. Learning to read got me a better job and more time to spend with my family." It is easy to tell that he is glad he took his wife's advice and overcame his difficulty with reading, but this is especially evident when he looks at his younger son, Jason.

His sons, James, age fourteen, and Jason, age nine, are engaging boys reaping the benefits of a close family. They are typical boys. James is quieter and chooses his words with the carefulness of a teenager, whereas Jason is quick to jump in. James enjoys kung fu and Jason plays soccer. Both like computer and video games. James excels in math and does well in school, but Jason, like his father, struggles with reading. However, he is quick to point out that his dad helps him at home, and he is doing much better now. Conquering Jason's difficulty with reading has been a challenge that the family has embraced, and Jason is showing steady improvement with the care and attention given to his reading from an early age. Even his older brother helps him.

"It's not like when I was growing up," Bev says. "Things are much better now. Jason goes to a reading tutor every Wednesday afternoon, and Saturdays he attends Reading Buddies at the library." Bev points out that his own difficulties with reading have made him all the more patient and understanding as a father, and happily, more involved in his sons' success.

Jason breaks in. "I have already finished my third novel this year and it is only October, and the book I'm reading now has sixty-five pages!" he exclaims wide-eyed. He is enthusiastic about reading, and this is obviously a source of joy for the whole family. "Sometimes," Jason tells me, "I read to my Mom, and I stop just before the exciting part, even when she asks me to keep going. I say, 'No, Mom, I'm making you wait just like my teacher makes me wait!'" There is obvious relish in leaving his mother at a cliffhanging moment, and everyone laughs. Sometimes, incentives are needed to encourage Jason to achieve the next level in his reading. Bev recalls that when a special Spider-Man camera was the reward earned, he willingly made the two-hour round trip drive "from Burtts Corner clear to Woodstock" to buy it for him.

The rewards for Bev in continuing to learn to read have been providing for his family, raising his boys in a learning environment, and being able to help them with school work. He is pleased to be able now to do the things that most people take for granted, such as reading the labels on medicine bottles. While Bev still struggles at times and continues with his tutor, reading and working toward literacy have brought many exciting moments.

He has been the recipient of some well-deserved honours. In 2003, he received the Sheree Fitch Adult Learner Scholarship. In 2005, Premier Bernard Lord presented Bev with a Council of the Federation Literacy Award certificate and medallion for his literacy achievements. CBC news covered the story. Jason takes great delight in re-watching the tape of this news item, filmed when a camera crew came to their house to interview Bev and to show him sitting at the kitchen table helping Jason learn to read.

When I ask the boys what their dad is good at besides reading, they both speak at once. "Dad can do almost anything!" says Jason. "At Youth Group, Dad helped me to build an aerodynamic car that won first prize, and he is helping James with a model for his French project. He paints our house, and he cooks eggs better than Mom!"

James is more reserved but no less enthusiastic. "Well, Dad is good at fixing things, you know, the stuff that you break. He's really fast at figuring things out. He just looks at it and tries to figure it out. If he can't fix it, he tries again until he can. He doesn't give up." James tells me that his father's approach to learning to read is like everything else he takes on in life. "If Dad can't do something, he keeps trying until he can, and if he still can't do it, he just tries some more." I can't help but think that his sons will do well with this example to follow.

His wife Krista's eyes fill with tears as she adds, "The boys are proud of him; we're all proud of him."

"Well, that's a big understatement, Mom," says James in true fourteen-year-old style. I glance at Bev, expecting to see embarrassment or perhaps the hint of tears. Instead he is looking off into the distance, nodding and smiling, clearly pleased with what the future holds for his family.

From the Hunger
ANGELA RANSON

The job for maintenance worker was posted in the lunch room. At the end
of my supper break, I heard one of the guys reading the description. That
job had better hours and better pay than mine with the cleaning crew at the
university. The same position had been posted before. I hadn't applied.

I went to school for the first time in September of 1970. I wasn't quite six
years old. I walked there with my brother, Jean-Paul. We left the house and
walked through the inner-city streets, passing the empty lot of tall waving
grass that no one mowed. We carried satchels filled with fresh notebooks and
pencils. No lunches.

There were crowds of kids at the school; I couldn't believe how many.
Why did there have to be so many kids? They were everywhere, and yet they
still didn't fill up the school. It was a huge building with so many rooms and
high ceilings. The light inside was pale and cloudy because it shone through
dirty windows.

The teacher was a tall, skinny girl with light skin and hair. She told me to
hang up my coat and satchel on one of the racks in the classroom, which I did.
The room smelled like wet cloth and old leather. Then I had to go inside and
sit at a desk. I didn't get what that was all about. Any time I had gone by the
school before, the kids had been outside, running and playing and shouting.

The teacher handed out books to read at home and a thin workbook that
would show us how to print. I didn't know as much as the other kids. They

could recite their *abc*'s and tie their shoelaces and tell the time and tell the difference between left and right. I didn't know that stuff. So when the bell rang and all the kids went outside to play at lunchtime, the teacher made me stay inside with her. Then she gave me extra work to do at home.

I didn't do it.

The next day the teacher asked me if I had my lessons done. I said no. She made me stay in at lunch again. I could see Jean-Paul waiting for me at the edge of the playground, watching the kids as they played. They didn't ask him to play, so Jean-Paul just stood there and watched. A hot, tight feeling growled in my chest and my stomach. It upset me, so I stood up and told the teacher I was going outside. She told me to sit down or I would have to stay after school, too.

I didn't sit down. The teacher kept me in after school, and Jean-Paul had to wait in the playground.

When she finally let me go, I ran outside to catch up with him and we started walking home. The hot, tight feeling made me mad all over again. As we passed the empty lot, I ripped open my satchel and flung my books into the tall grass. There went the reading book. There went my scribblers. There went my writing booklet. There went my pencils and erasers. Jean-Paul watched me throw them away one by one.

"Roger, why did you do that?" he asked.

"I don't need 'em," I answered. "I ain't going back to that place. Ever."

We got to our house and climbed the wooden steps. It was a big house, green paint peeling from the boards. We dropped our satchels on the floor by the door and walked in through the living room and back to the kitchen, where we knew Mum would be.

She was standing at the stove, stirring some soup in a pot. Dad must have brought home groceries after all. He had been out the night before, so we had thought he would forget again. Jean-Paul told her that I had thrown away my books.

"Why did you do that?" she asked, although the words weren't clear. Her top lip didn't meet in the middle, so her words always came out strangely. It didn't matter to us. We always understood her anyway.

I folded my arms. "I ain't going back there," I declared.

She pushed back a piece of black hair that had fallen over her forehead. "You have to go back."

"No, I don't. I'll just stay here with you."

"You ain't staying here. You have to go to school."

"But I can't do anything, and they ain't helping me. Will you help me?"

She let go of the spoon and wrapped her arms around herself, as if she was giving herself a hug. "I ain't helping. That's a teacher's job. They're supposed to help with that stuff, not me."

I went back. I never did get the hang of reading, but I got real good at printing. I got real good at talking, too, and I could remember everything and count things up. I would count for my mother sometimes, when she took me to the Met for clothes. I would talk for her, too, when the cashier didn't understand her. Sometimes, we would go to Deluxe French Fries and I would order. She didn't like going out too much, though, and we almost never had the money for Deluxe.

By the time I headed for middle school, I was used to being hungry. My father was out more often than he was home, and he didn't always remember to save some of his paycheque for food, even though he always cashed his cheques at the grocery store. The management there let him sign with an *X*.

Mum got sick when I was ten, and Dad was drinking too much to take care of us, so Jean-Paul and I were sent to a foster home in Rexton. We didn't get put in school right away because they didn't know how long we were going to have to stay. The woman who took us was strict, very strict. She wouldn't let us anywhere in the house but in our bedroom or in the kitchen. We only got to eat once her kids had finished, and we had to take baths together to save on water. We were there three weeks, and all the time that growling inside me got louder and louder.

One Saturday the woman's kids were watching cartoons, so we went in to watch them, too. We had always watched cartoons at home. Once the kids saw us in the living room, they told us we weren't allowed in there. Then their mother came in and ordered us back into the kitchen. I got mad and so she sent us into our bedroom. I said to Jean-Paul that we should just crawl out the window and run away, but he was too afraid. He even told the woman on me, and she came upstairs all mad, but she didn't scare me. "I want to talk to the social worker."

"No."

"If you don't let me talk to the social worker, I'm going to burn this whole place down."

She laughed at me. "And how are you going to manage that?"

"I'll use the electrical system."

I got to talk to the social worker, and I told her that I'd rather go home alone than stay in that place. She said she'd come and get me in a day or two.

I went home, but Mum was still too sick to take care of me, so I ended up in another foster home two weeks later. I told the social worker I could take care of myself and Jean-Paul, too, but she didn't agree. She left Jean-Paul in Rexton and took me to stay with a lady named Jean, who recognized me from the Nazarene Church. I saw some pictures on her mantel of people I knew from the church, too. Jean was a good foster mother. After my mother died, she became my mother, and all of the foster kids that were with her became my sisters and brothers. Even Jean-Paul loved Jean, although he never lived with her like I did. I stayed there for eight years, until I was old enough to live on my own.

Jean-Paul and I got sick of watching the kids in the playground at middle school, so we joined the Army Cadets for something else to do. It wasn't too bad a way to spend Friday nights. I was good in the training, but I couldn't do the tests for rifles and things like that. One of the warrant officers asked me if I was stupid during a test once, and I said I just had trouble with reading and writing. The other cadets thought that was funny, but the warrant officer said he would just ask me the questions. I got too nervous to answer, so I flunked anyway. The other cadets started treating me like I had a disease. I started to wonder if they were right. It made me mad, so I got good at war games.

I joined the cadet band, because they didn't take the same tests. I played the drums because I couldn't read notes. The other guys in the band still called me names. One of the sergeants spit in my face when we were on a bus one night. I told the warrant officer, and we ended up having a meeting in the captain's office. The guy apologized so that I wouldn't have him kicked out.

I went to Gagetown for a two-week camp soon after I started high school and learned about maps, shooting, and drills. I still didn't know my left and right, but a lot of the girls said I was doing really well. That was nice. Then I got the rank of corporal. I learned my left and right real quick then, because I had to lead the parades. I didn't want to look stupid when I was giving out the commands. I had to do a lot more tests and a lot more writing once I made corporal, though, so I quit soon after that. It was getting too hard.

All through high school, I told the teachers that I had a hard time reading and that they should leave me alone. They did and I graduated. I still couldn't read, but I was already earning my own money. I had a job at McKay's Dairy, loading ice cream onto the frozen food truck. I figured out what the symbols on the boxes meant, so that I always loaded the right stuff.

After graduation, I didn't want to do that anymore, but I couldn't do much else. I looked into joining the army for combat training, but they said they didn't have anything for me. At that time, twenty thousand people were being laid off from the Armed Forces. I didn't know where else to go or what else I could do. I was good at following orders, though. I would have been a good soldier.

Finally I went to the UIC (employment) office and asked the woman there for help. I told her I couldn't read.

"How can you have a diploma if you can't read? You must be awful stupid."

I didn't like her. But she took me upstairs to see a lady who was very nice.

She asked me what skills I had and what I was good at. Then she got me into this program that I found out later was for people who are "slow" or "retarded."

She filled in the application form for me and got me a job with Bordeaux Maintenance. I ended up cleaning at Champlain Place. They actually showed me how to clean bathrooms, wash floors, sweep, and clean windows. I thought it was a real joke, until I saw my paycheque: $130 for two weeks' full-time work. Then it wasn't so funny.

I went to Saint John after two years with Bordeaux. I got a job at Ocean Janitor Service with a friend of mine and started making better money. I worked at Market Square, fourteen hours a day, for about a year. I also worked in offices on the side. My boss, Raoul, and I got to be good friends. He said I was one of his best workers. He expanded the business into Prince Edward Island and Moncton, and I went there sometimes to help him out. I met my wife, Lisa, when I was in Moncton. We got married in 1989. I got a job cleaning at the university and relocated to Moncton. Soon after, the job for maintenance worker came up the first time. I didn't apply.

The first time the maintenance job was posted, my father was still alive. He was living in a basement apartment on Maple Street with Dot, his girlfriend. He had left Mum when I was about twelve, and she died soon after. Dot could read and write, and she taught him to write his name. I remember watching Dad write a G and feeling so impressed — Dad could write his name. We were all amazed. Dot didn't teach him much else. He stopped driving a garbage truck for the city and started driving a delivery truck. He used to lie when he had to read a piece of paper for a job and say he'd forgotten his glasses, so that he could get someone else to read for him.

In the spring of 1991, Jean-Paul called me and said that Dad was real sick, and he wanted to get together with us to talk. My wife came with me, and we met at the apartment. Dad didn't get up when we got there. He already looked grey and thin, and he knew he didn't have long. So he talked about his funeral, about the life insurance he had from his work. It was in the names of us kids so he wanted to make sure we divided it up evenly and helped Dot out with the funeral costs. We promised that we would.

Dad told us that he was sorry he hadn't been there for us when we were kids. He said that he knew he hadn't been much of a father. It was the first time he had ever said he was sorry for all the days we went to school without lunches or came home to nothing for supper, for all the drinking, for giving us up to foster care, for leaving Mum. Then he said he loved us. That was quite a blow for me. I had walked into that place angry and hurt, sure that because he had never shown fatherly love and concern he had never felt it. But he did love us, and he said so. Then he told us that he wished he had done more for himself so that he could have done more for us, but it was too late. He had lung and brain cancer, probably from the alcohol and cigarettes.

He wanted us to forgive him before he was gone. I forgave him right then, and I wanted to talk to him about what we could do in the time we had left. I told him it wasn't too late yet. We could still get together, do father-and-son things. Family things. We planned a barbecue before we all left that day. Dad always liked to do things outdoors.

Dot called me first when Dad had his stroke just a few weeks after our talk. I told her to call the ambulance and get him to the hospital, which she did. I went to visit him. He had never been well enough for that barbecue we talked about. He died just a few days later.

And then the maintenance job was posted again. As the guy in the lunch room read the description, I could hear Dad's voice saying he wished he had done more for himself. I still remembered that growling in my stomach from when I was a kid. I remembered my mother, trying to figure out how much the food at Deluxe cost. I knew by then that she didn't know how to read or write either, which is why she couldn't help me any more than my father had been able to help me. But I could help myself.

I went to Laubach Literacy and got a tutor and found out that my reading was at a grade two level. I started working with my tutor, and then I applied for the job. I told them that I couldn't read well enough to do it yet, but I was going to learn. I promised that I would do a good job if they gave me the chance.

They gave me the chance. And I grabbed it.

Creating a Future
WENDY KITTS

Karen, a thirty-three-year-old single mother living in Moncton, "wasn't really into school" the first time around. Born and raised in Toronto, she took a part-time job in grade nine at a daycare, something that pleased her parents. "That was really important to my family — to work," explains Karen who, like other kids her age, wanted money for clothes or movies. "They really pressured me to make sure I went to work."

Although her mother recognized the value of an education and encouraged Karen to finish school, her father felt her job should take precedence. Despite differing opinions, they agreed that her position at the daycare held great promise and provided a way for Karen to pay for the things she wanted. The job quickly became Karen's priority, and the required hours both before and after school sometimes made her late for class.

Towards the end of grade ten, Karen found herself suspended from school because of her tardiness. As a condition to returning to class, the principal demanded she obtain six credits from a high school in a neighbouring community. Karen felt the ruling was unacceptable. To earn the extra credits, she would have had to travel by bus a half-hour each way, thereby extending her school day, something that would interfere with her already tight work schedule. Since quitting her job was not an option she would consider, Karen decided to quit school instead and work full time at the daycare.

Over the next few years, she prospered both professionally and financially in her position, earning close to $18 an hour. "I was like a teacher. I was making good money at a young age. I ended up moving out, getting my own place." But it didn't last. Through sweeping changes to the Ontario daycare system, Karen's non-profit centre became unionized. As a result of government cutbacks and her low seniority, her work hours were reduced to just a couple per day. "That just wasn't going to cut it," remembers Karen, who was devastated by the turn of events and unsure as to what she would do. "I had bills. I had a car, my own apartment. I wasn't able to afford it."

Chance intervened and her career took a different direction when she landed an office job through a friend's father. "I got really lucky," says Karen, who thrived at her new position. She learned new skills related to accounting and customer service. But then a few years later, a change in the company's ownership once again threatened her job security. "They [the new owners] wanted to change things. They let me go and I was devastated. I was like, 'What am I going to do now?'"

Karen turned to waitressing for the short-term. She eventually secured another office position as a head hunter, helping other people find jobs. Once again, she excelled at her job, soaking up even more business skills and knowledge. "I had a great boss. I really shined at that company," recalls Karen, who opened a new location while she was employed there. "I helped build the company from the bottom up. Then," she pauses, "I found out I was pregnant."

In December of 2006, Karen gave birth to her daughter, Emma. Although her boss encouraged her to return to her position after her maternity leave, she decided she wanted to be closer to her family — most of whom lived in New Brunswick. "After having my daughter, I really felt I was on my own and too far away from my family, so I thought it was time for a change." In June 2007, Karen and Emma moved to Hopewell Cape, New Brunswick, to live with one of Karen's sisters, while Karen sought work in the Moncton area.

Finding a job on the East Coast proved difficult. Karen was repeatedly asked if she had graduated from high school — something that was never an issue before and a question she had always managed to side-step during interviews in Toronto. "It was something I was so insecure about, so I'd do anything I could to avoid the question or talk around it. There were times I would lie and say that I had it," explains Karen, who had never even discussed it with her family. "I felt really ashamed. I chose not to admit to it and be in denial."

The question could not be evaded in Moncton, however, where Karen was often asked to produce a copy of her diploma. "In Ontario, I'd never been asked for it. Down here they want to see it, to pump gas they want a copy of your diploma," she laughs. "I was like, 'What am I going to do? How am I going to get a job?'"

Determined to make a new life for herself and Emma, Karen decided to get her GED diploma. She ordered the text books (which came from Ontario, ironically), prepaid the testing fee, and booked a date to write the two-day GED exam six weeks later.

When the books arrived late, a mere two weeks before the exam, Karen panicked. She did not know how she could possibly study the huge amount of material required in such a short time, especially as most of her time was taken up with Emma. "I went through the book every time she went down for a nap and every night after she went to bed," she says. "While she was in the bath, I sat in the bathroom reading the book and doing the questionnaires."

Karen managed to study four of the five necessary modules — all except the math section. "I wasn't able to wrap my head around that at all. I didn't have time," she says, knowing she would forfeit the exam fee if she didn't write the test as planned. "I was a nervous wreck, but I went and I did the exam. I had no choice. I can't live down here if I can't find work. I had to go, I couldn't extend it. So I wrote it anyways."

When the test results arrived in the mail a couple of weeks later, Karen was elated to discover that she had passed everything but the one module she had not studied — math. Knowing she would need some help with this subject, Karen inquired about tutoring and was directed to a government-funded CALP centre in Salisbury — an hour-long drive from her home, which was by then in Hillsborough.

She was happily surprised to learn of the help available in New Brunswick for people like her, people who had a desire to upgrade their learning and skills to create a better future for themselves. Karen learned she qualified for financial assistance through the Training & Skills Development program under the Department of Post-Secondary Education, Training and Labour to help with the costs of Emma's daycare while she prepared for her GED exam.

. For the next six weeks, she spent two hours a day travelling to and from the CALP centre, putting in eight hours a day, five days a week studying math. To help her with her weak language arts skills, Karen's teacher suggested she attend a public speaking seminar held by the LCNB. The workshop, along with her daily classroom experience, gave her much-needed confidence, and she realized she was not alone in her struggle to learn. "I met a lot of people in the same boat as me who didn't have their grade twelve, so it was nice because for so long this was a big secret," explains Karen who felt an immediate bond with the other students she met through the centre. "One thing that came out of this is discovering other people from all walks of life, all ages, with as many reasons for not finishing school. We all had different levels and goals of what we wanted, what we were going for."

Karen's unwavering goal was to secure a better future for Emma and herself. She wanted to develop a career, establish a long-term plan instead of grasping the short-term goal of just getting a job, any job. Through TSD, she explored her options with a career counsellor. "We narrowed it down, and it came back to my roots — early childhood education!" Karen was thrilled to realize how her first job at the daycare and her subsequent office jobs, where she acquired both business and customer service skills, would be the foundation for her new career. It was suggested that she might even open her own daycare someday. "That just set me off," says Karen excitedly. "I'm very business-oriented, and I would like to be part of children's lives and create a future for them."

Her next step was to research this possible career path and discover which organizations might hire her and what level of education they would require. "I did my homework," says Karen, "to make sure this was something I really wanted to do." She also investigated various schools and programs to find out which one could provide the training best suited for her needs. She decided upon NBCC's Early Childhood Education program. Two factors determined her decision: the one-year certificate program could be transferred towards university credits if required, and it offered business courses on owning and operating a daycare — an element crucial to her long-term plan.

Karen still had a couple of hurdles to overcome. Applying to NBCC required a high school diploma, something she still did not have. Although she was scheduled to rewrite her GED in August, school started in September, so if she waited to apply after she had her diploma, it would be too late and she'd have to wait another year. Impatient to make her dream happen, Karen struck a deal with the college administrators to allow her to apply to NBCC without her diploma on the condition that she would have to have her GED before she could graduate. Finally, the only thing left standing between Karen and her dream was funding.

TSD had agreed to pay half of her tuition, her books, and a portion of Emma's daycare services but only if Karen completed her GED first. Refusing to give up after coming so far, she convinced TSD that she had as much to lose financially as they did if she didn't get her GED because she had borrowed the money needed to cover her share of the costs from a family member. "I was determined because my daughter really made me realize that I want to set a good example for her when she grows up," explains Karen. "I can say, 'Listen, your mom was able to provide and be somebody and be educated, because with technology if you're not educated, you're in trouble. You'll be in a dead-end job or going from job to job like I did.'"

The hard work and steadfast commitment were rewarded. In August 2008, Karen made good on her promise and obtained her GED. Also as promised, both TSD and NBCC supported her in attending the College's ECE program in September.

Not wanting to lose any more time, she is already researching funding possibilities to assist her in opening her own daycare (preferably a non-profit centre) in Albert County after she graduates. "I'm hoping by the time I'm done school all this paperwork will be done," explains Karen who has already made a lot of contacts in the daycare business. "I feel it's time for me to contribute and get back to my roots and open up a learning centre."

Karen feels she's close to attaining her goals, and she credits CALP for providing the necessary tools and motivation for changing her life. "The literacy program gave me confidence to stand up and tell my story. It gave me a wonderful teacher, who got me in contact with the literacy coalition, which gave me confidence to go after my goals, to believe in myself, to see that there are other people in the same boat," she explains. "I've learned that it's okay to go back to school at any age."

She is enjoying school much more this time around despite being older than most of her classmates. "I love everyone in my class," she gushes. "I'm the mother hen and we all get along great. Everyone is respectful, and I wouldn't have had that confidence before."

Karen's confidence was born of her dogged determination to make a better life for Emma and herself and to obtain her GED. "Once I had the GED . . . what a weight off my shoulders!" she says proudly. "I'm not going to say it was easy, but I knew I had to [do it]. If I wanted to stay in New Brunswick, if I wanted to be with my family, if I wanted my daughter to have a better way of life here as opposed to what I had in Ontario, I had to — I knew I had to."

"I used to think 'If this job doesn't work out, I'll just get another.' Now I've got a career. I'm happy now. I have a future. I have goals, stuff I didn't have before. I believe I created my future. I went to meetings, I called people on the phone, I studied, I made plans for the test — I did all that. I made arrangements to get a ride. I made arrangements for someone to watch my daughter — I made it happen," stresses Karen. "That's half the battle, making it happen . . . and I did."

A Parachute for Ralph

RICHARD DOIRON

"So this is what it feels like to free-fall at over a hundred miles an hour! Thank God for the parachute!"

Ralph had just jumped out of an airplane. Many people would consider this an extremely bold move, but Ralph is not most people. Born January 2, 1961, one of thirteen children, the Wolfville, Nova Scotia, native and former resident has been jumping out of a different kind of plane for most of his life, and there has been no parachute.

For much of his life, Ralph was functionally illiterate. By 2007, he had become a proficient reader, and his determination had been so pronounced that he had received special recognition. He could choose his prize, so he chose skydiving. That day, in September 2007, he could look back on his life with distinct pride. In so many ways he was on top of the world.

"I was a slow learner," says Ralph. "But other children (mostly from higher grades) labelled me. 'Retard' was one of the hurtful words they used. There were other names too, but that one really sticks out . . . I was in a special class, but it wasn't good. We weren't assigned much to do. In fact, we were encouraged to watch cartoons on a TV set up in the classroom, and we watched shows like *Hogan's Heroes* and *Gilligan's Island*."

Watching basic TV fare was one thing, grasping concepts quite another. When something new was thrown at him, Ralph struggled. The process had to be repeated numerous times. It took patience. Admittedly, he didn't always have enough of that. Neither did others. And some resorted to taunts. Beyond the ensuing hurt, confusion and self-doubt mounted.

In winter, Ralph and others in the class went skating. While that was good, it was not something to build a future on. He even recalls getting hit over the head with a chair wielded by another classmate. "It was like sitting at a card table and always being dealt bad hands. It was very frustrating."

In addition to the difficulties at school, Ralph went through a series of half a dozen foster homes, his parents having gone their separate ways when he was five years old. In some of those homes he was abused, both emotionally and physically; in at least one instance, he was beaten to welts. In that case, a teacher had picked up on his plight and he had been promptly moved elsewhere. He was moved physically, but the emotional scars remained, running much deeper than the flesh wounds.

Ralph was promoted regularly, and he finally made it to grade nine. In effect, though, the grades were bogus. There was one thing in his life that was special then, however, and that was his involvement in the Air Cadets. He spent five years in the cadets and attained the rank of corporal. As a result, he entertained dreams of a career in the military, but those dreams did not materialize. In the cadets, Ralph had earned his stripes through oral testing. Regular Forces didn't go that route. He had also managed to acquire a hunter safety certificate through oral testing, and he felt undeniable pride in that achievement. In retrospect, he admits that every success, no matter how small it might have seemed to anyone else, represented a milestone to him as a boy and became his incentive to try even harder.

More than two decades ago, prior to moving to Moncton from Nova Scotia, Ralph worked at a number of odd jobs. Included in those were stints in a lumberyard as well as in a chicken slaughterhouse. In Moncton, he resided in and worked at a trailer park, where he did clean-up work. While living there, he witnessed his share of human tragedies. He also got himself into some legal trouble. Though his skirmishes with the law were mostly minor, he experienced another downside to the binds of illiteracy. Legal Aid, with all of its inadequacies, would be his only defence, and he spent short stints behind bars.

Understandably, it was easy to feel frustrated. There were times when employers were inconsiderate. In fact, there were times when some regarded Ralph as less important than themselves. Raises were not forthcoming. On one occasion, a supervisor told him straight out that he wasn't smart. Ralph was angry over such poor treatment. "I said to him, 'So you don't think I'm smart, eh, well here's how smart I am — I quit!" Of course, quitting was also a setback. There had to be better options.

Ralph became involved in activities with the Moncton Boys & Girls Club. It was there that someone suggested he give literacy training a shot. An interview was set up with a literacy tutor. He was hopeful, but that tutor didn't show up, a mystery still. It amounted to another disappointment. He persevered. The next tutor showed and offered invaluable help for five years.

Achieving literacy was an absolute godsend: "Literacy gave me enough confidence and courage to eventually get a laptop and teach myself how to use it." Ralph made such inroads with this technology that, during a literacy conference at the University of Moncton in 2005, he substituted for a computer lab instructor when the teacher could not attend.

One year after his skydiving experience, Ralph has a second tutor. Peter is a celebrated literacy advocate and tutor with Laubach Literacy. He has more than thirty years of volunteer work under his belt. Ralph meets with Peter one day each week, and he has nothing but praise for him and for all the people who work with the disadvantaged. In fact, along the way he saw fit to get involved in the very process himself.

The LCNB presented Ralph with an Achievement Award in the summer of 2008. He proudly reads aloud the inscription: "Completed training in Public Speaking and Media Relations sponsored by the Literacy Coalition of New Brunswick and became a member of the SOUL Speakers Bureau."

Between deft displays on his laptop, he explains how he functions as student representative for the whole province of New Brunswick with

Laubach Literacy. He is also student president for the local support group. He works to recruit both students and literacy volunteers. "I want to help others the way I've been helped. I sit on local council, student council, and provincial council. I help others who are interested in learning computer skills. I know what it's like to sit in a corner and say nothing . . . no voice . . . like you don't matter. The thing is that we all matter. And when we can, we need to step up to the plate."

Ralph continues to fight an uphill battle. Five years ago a literacy test gave him a grade three reading level. He harbours no illusions. Still, his mantra is, "You can't get anything better when you can't read," and he has a noble goal, too: he wants to get his mechanic's licence. That's still a long way down the road, however, and he knows it. "I can't say that I'll be getting my GED certificate in any specific timeframe. Also, there is the mechanic's course itself. That takes a couple years to complete. At my age, some are inclined to say it might be hard to get work even with a certificate, but I need to believe in something . . . my goal . . . that simple."

Not yet deemed functionally literate, Ralph's finances and sense of autonomy are typically limited. "I live on Income Assistance," he says. "It's not easy. I fall under the disabled category. It's a reality I have to deal with. Hopefully, that will change, and I will have a better standard of living. In the meantime, I will continue with my education and continue to help others. I have been able to make a lot of friends in a lot of places around the globe. I've got a lot of stuff to learn on the computer yet, but I'm constantly learning. I wanted so badly to be like other people, you know, to be able to write. Let's face it, a few years ago I couldn't have done this for a number of reasons, including lack of confidence."

The gravity of Ralph's words is difficult to imagine for anyone who has been functionally literate all along, until one sees the gleam in his eyes as he makes his position known and then proceeds to give a demonstration on his laptop. He shows the games he plays on Xbox, a video game console produced by Microsoft. He eagerly explains how the small tower can be used like a computer and inserts a disk to play a short film. Playing the games helps him further master language. The games, after all, have directions. "It's kind of like driving a car. You can't just get into a car and drive it. Everything is a system."

So what does the future hold for Ralph? Well, he certainly is no longer jumping without a parachute. Astutely, he makes the connection between literacy and skydiving: "Going through life not able to read was a lot like not having a parachute. You know when I jumped out of that plane [after a brief training session], the jump was done in tandem. The instructor was behind me and the one to pull the cord. I felt confident that he knew what he was doing. Being able to read gives me confidence, too. When a person can read, it's their safety net."

Ralph knows he has come a long way. He also knows that there will always be challenges ahead. But, then, he once jumped out of an airplane without hesitation, and that, too, sets him apart. Most people would never have dared.

Soaring
AFIENA KAMMINGA

Cathy looks younger than her forty-four years. Her sturdy, capable hands rest quietly in her lap as she talks with a strong, deep voice, unexpected in a woman so petite. She talks about the day, six years ago, when her teenage daughters encouraged her to take free upgrading courses offered by the local CALP, insisting that it is never too late to learn. It took every ounce of Cathy's courage to make the initial phone call and to go in for the assessment. What if she truly was incapable of learning? What if she was headed for yet another failure?

She had spent her years in the public school system at the back of the class, wondering why the other students knew how to read and do math when she did not; why they knew the answers to the questions the teachers asked, and she did not. After eight years of feeling helpless, frustrated, bewildered, and outright stupid much of the time, Cathy left school unable to read and write. And she left wondering why she couldn't learn to do these things.

When she went to CALP, Cathy learned from the assessment that she had dyslexia, a neurological condition that causes letters and figures to change form and position on the page. She also discovered that people with dyslexia tend to be bright and have excellent memories, since they rely on their memorizing skills to compensate for their inability to read.

All the same, she faced many challenges in daily life. Take shopping for food — Cathy accomplished her grocery shopping guided only by the pictures or colouring on the package. Dealing with prescription medications — her own or a loved one's — without help from the label left her feeling stressed and frustrated. Even though she did pass her driver's test, after being thoroughly prepared by her literacy mentor, she still found it difficult to read street signs or a city map.

Cathy's assessment convinced her that she could succeed in achieving her literacy goals. Knowing that she was not "too stupid to learn" provided the basis for a new and growing self-confidence. There was, she then knew, a physiological reason why she had not been able to read, write, and do math, and it had nothing to do with lack of intelligence. At CALP, she met other people who had their own story to tell about why they were back at school. She was not alone.

She mustered all her pluck to tackle once again the mysteries of letters and figures, their meaning, and how they fit together — things that had eluded her many years ago. As she progressed in the literacy program, her world began to change dramatically.

Three years into the program, Cathy received a New Brunswick Alpha Award medal in recognition of her remarkable progress. The entire class travelled to Fredericton to attend the medal presentation and to hear Cathy's acceptance speech. It was the first time she was called upon to speak in public. She was, understandably, shaking at the thought of addressing a room filled with dignitaries, teachers, family, and friends. Still, when her turn came, she pulled herself together and spoke with confidence and sincerity.

There have been other rewards. Cathy's literacy has helped to improve the lives of her family members. The one-on-one life skills coaching offered by the CALP instructor enabled Cathy to advocate on behalf of her son, who had run into difficulties at school. She has learned to navigate the social assistance bureaucracy more effectively, and she no longer gets lost when driving on her own through an unfamiliar neighbourhood or town. These days, when her aging parents call upon her to drive them to medical appointments, she is able to say yes with full confidence. She helps them out when they have trouble reading the directions on their prescription labels. She assists them in their dealings with medical professionals and helps them to make decisions involving their health care.

While she is proud of her medal and her hard-won life skills, Cathy's enthusiasm bubbles to the surface when she talks about her greatest achievement.

After years on welfare with no hope of earning a decent wage, she is now able to work at a full-time job, an accomplishment that leaves her filled with a buoyant feeling of self-worth. The greatest difference between her present and preliterate days, she stresses, lies in the satisfaction of having a job and earning her keep. Being able to contribute to society in a meaningful way has given her a whole new sense of dignity.

A great deal of tenacity and patience from Cathy and her teacher helped in achieving these life-changing results. Cathy faced significant challenges trying to balance classes, part-time work, and home life, responding to one demand after another. In addition to classes five mornings a week, she had an afternoon job. Evenings were hectic as well. There was no time to relax between doing housework and supervising her children — time well spent, two of her children graduated from high school.

People who know Cathy say that over the last six years, she has experienced a metamorphosis. She has emerged from the bleakness of supporting three children through part-time jobs and social assistance to a life of self-sufficiency. She has grown from a labouring caterpillar to a soaring butterfly. The new Cathy has emerged knowing her worth, laughing and smiling, meeting your gaze when she speaks. She is determined to continue her flight to ever new heights.

The Hardest Thing I Ever Did

DAWN WATSON

It was the hardest thing I ever did.

There I was sitting in the car outside Canadian Tire, gripping the wheel so hard it's a wonder I didn't snap it in two. Not that I'm such a strong man. I'm not a strong man; I like to think of myself as compact. But it's a wonder I didn't break that wheel. I suppose my two fists had never shaken with such force.

The windshield was covered with ice, inside and out. The heater was gone again. All the way into town that morning, I had to stop every ten minutes to scrape the windshield, both outside and in. I had come into town early for my lessons that morning. I was learning to read because I wanted to be able to help my little girl, Felicia, with her school work, and I wanted to read her stories. I had been working hard for two years by that time, but I still had a long way to go.

It was just a few days before Christmas, and I still hadn't got Felicia's present. She's a young lady now, but she was a little girl then, and I didn't have her present yet. Oh, I had some stuff from the Dollar Store, but she had her heart set on Polly Pocket's Dream Home. She had written a letter to Santa Claus and asked him for it.

Polly Pocket's Dream Home was in Canadian Tire. That present was under the counter in there. The woman with the big diamond ring and a lot of pins on her shirt put it there when she took away my credit card. I had no money. I used the last of it to put gas in the car that morning. I would get that back; the government paid my gas money to get to my lessons. By then, it would be too late. Christmas would be over.

I was stuck. I wanted to get that present for Felicia, and at the same time, I didn't know how I was going to go back in there and get it. I started thinking about what my teacher had said that morning. I was going to write a letter to myself as homework, and I was addressing the envelope. So far, I had printed everything. I asked my teacher if I could *write* my name, and she said sure. She told me I did a good job.

This was my chance to ask something I'd often wondered about. "Look," I said to her while I wrote my name on the page of my scribbler. "It looks different from the one I put on the envelope. It looks different every time I write it. Why is that?" She said that I wasn't really writing my name since I couldn't *write* each of the letters. She said I was really drawing a picture, and if I tried to draw pictures of a tree, each one would look a little different.

When I left, she wished me a merry Christmas. I remembered that, sitting in my car with no heater thinking, not much chance of that now. Canadian Tire was crowded. I should have done my shopping earlier. I don't like crowds; I'm kind of shy. I had shopped there lots of times with my card. I bought what I needed, and then I would pay off the card later. Maybe if I'd shopped earlier, I might have passed Felicia's present and my card to someone else.

But I had shopped that day, and the diamond ring woman put it under the counter and took my card. First she got me to sign a paper, and then she looked at my card. She told me to sign my name on a different piece of paper. By this time, people were lined up at the front desk behind me, and I could tell they were all listening. I didn't know what was wrong, but I was embarrassed just the same. I wrote my name again and she stared at it and at my card through her granny glasses. "That's not your signature!" she made sure she was loud enough for everyone to hear.

She put Felicia's present under the counter and put my card under the cash register. Then she reached around me to take the presents from the next person in line. We were done. And that was why I was sitting, freezing in my car a few days before Christmas, holding onto that wheel like there was no tomorrow, except there was a tomorrow, and only a few more of them before Christmas.

I was thinking of how Felicia had helped me decorate the tree, or I had helped her, really. Whatever she couldn't reach she told me to do, and she made sure I followed her orders to the last branch and twig. When we were satisfied with our work, we made popcorn, and I told her how God sent His Son to us to teach us how we should live. We sat in front of the tree, and we didn't even turn the TV on. We talked about the Christmas story and how much God must love us to send us His Son.

As a single parent, I worried that I didn't give her everything she needed to grow up to be the best she could be. That's part of the reason I had to learn to read. I wanted her to be able to get a good job so she could afford to have a car with a heater that works, so she would have money left at the end of the month, so she could have a big diamond ring if she wanted one. I wanted her to be able to write and not just draw pictures.

I wanted her life to be better than mine. And I wanted her life to be as good — for her to someday have a child to bring her joy. After I stewed for a while, it became very clear what I needed to do.

The hardest thing I ever did was let go of that wheel. I got out of the car and walked across the parking lot. I was shivering, and I didn't think it was because of the weather. I got in line at the desk, not at the regular cash registers. The lines were shorter now, and the lady with the pins was doing what she usually does, helping people who didn't like what they got. I didn't like what I got, so I was in the right line. I practised my speech to her over and over until it was my turn. Then my speech disappeared, but I told her I wanted to talk to the boss. Once again, everyone was staring at me.

Finally, the boss came, and he asked how he could help me. The words were like sharp little stones in my mouth as I said, "I'm just learning how to read, and my teacher says my name doesn't look the same every time I write it because I'm just drawing a picture." Now everyone was staring *and* listening. The boss put his arm around my shoulder, and he took me to a section that wasn't full of people. He listened to what I had to say, how I was addressing an envelope that day and how I had asked my teacher why my name looked different every time I wrote it and how the lady with the glasses had taken my card away and that was why Felicia's present was under the counter.

The boss told me he admired me for learning to read. He wanted to shake my hand. I shook his hand, but just then I was still waiting to see if I'd get Felicia's present. It wasn't until after I got home that the moment sank in: the boss of a big store wanted to shake my hand because he admired me.

I did get the Polly Pocket Dream Home, the boss made sure of that, and Christmas was wonderful. Felicia was so happy with her gift, and that night when I tucked her in, I saw a lump underneath the covers. It was the Dream Home and all the Polly Pockets she owned.

In January, when I went to my next lessons, I told my teacher all about sitting in the car and talking to the boss and wrapping Felicia's gift. She was quiet for a little bit, just looking at me. Then she said, "Raymond, you are my hero."

Family Comes First

LAURIE GLENN NORRIS

For Myrtle, family is everything. This feisty Maliseet woman does not hesitate to speak her mind about the importance of child-rearing and families sticking together. "You don't gain anything by sending your kids away," she shakes her head. "I never had much — I'm no angel — but I looked after the kids first." Myrtle learned this the hard way, first as a child whose early life was a series of moves and later as an adult with children of her own to look after.

Myrtle, who never knew her biological parents, was born in the Saint John Hospital and as a young child lived with her brother and sister at an orphanage on the Shubenacadie Indian Reserve. When she was about nine years old, she was brought to Fredericton to live with foster mother Annie Paul, who raised her and whom she calls "mother." Today, at seventy-one, Myrtle lives on the St. Mary's Reserve, on Fredericton's north side.

Along with family, she is also strongly committed to helping those less fortunate than she. "I was taught — see a hungry person, feed them. Today everything is so unreal." Myrtle is an attractive woman with short grey hair, twinkling brown eyes, and a smile that belies her years. She raised four sons and a daughter and is now helping to bring up her grandchildren. She is fiercely proud of them all. The walls of her cozy living room are filled with their photographs and mementos. One son is a United States Marine; her only daughter has two girls. "She's a good mother — strict. I told her, 'Don't be too strict.'"

Myrtle grew up in a household of twelve children. "We didn't know what fun was. There were so many of us, we didn't have much." She remembers her sister and Annie Paul making wreaths out of tree boughs just before

Christmas. She and her younger brother would sell them door-to-door at night. "I remember walking over the old bridge with those wreaths."

Annie Paul could not read or write, and Myrtle didn't learn to either. "Lots of people couldn't in those days," she says. She has a photograph from her days at a Native day school. Myrtle is standing in the back row, one of the eldest. School was where Myrtle learned the alphabet and numbers. "We were taught by Catholic nuns," she says. "I remember cleaning bathrooms a lot. My mother got mad. She said if I needed to do housecleaning I could do that at home. I don't think they taught us very much. They tried to teach us knitting. I felt I didn't belong there."

In all, her formal schooling amounted to about three years. From an early age, her focus was work. "I thought about it all the time. Work was a way to explain myself," she says. "I didn't want to stay around and sponge off people, bother people. I'm a survivor. My mother always told me, 'We all have to survive in our own way.'"

Myrtle describes herself as a lifelong scrapper. "There wasn't one fight I couldn't handle as a young person. Any boy tried to mess with me, I'd say, 'You got hold of the wrong girl!' I would always knock the boys down."

When Myrtle was thirteen, she and two friends left Fredericton for the United States. They went to Boston and worked for a time in a linen factory, dipping delicate tablecloths and doilies in starch so they would retain their shape. "When we got paid, it was a big deal. We thought we had a thousand dollars," she says, laughing at the memory. Myrtle and her friends didn't stay in any one place long. They would return to Fredericton for a few months and then leave again. She explains how they got jobs. "People thought we were older than we were 'cause we were tall."

It was difficult for her, living and trying to get around in a big city after Fredericton. "It was awkward. One of the girls was smart; she helped us." Myrtle travelled in Boston mostly by riding the subway and walking. She wasn't able to read the names of destinations on buses or subway trains or on street signs. "I would mark down names of the places that I had to go. I would follow people, watch where they went. After a while I learned." She used to count the number of blocks she had walked and memorize the directions she had taken. "I had a hard time with the right and the left," she recalls. She knew she would have to do the whole thing in reverse to get back home.

She met her husband in New Haven, Connecticut. They were together for seven years. It was an abusive relationship. "We never went anywhere; I felt like a prisoner. He was an Irishman with a bad temper. I used to call him a party animal. He was not a family man — he didn't want to bother with the kids." She worked on a farm owned by her husband's family. "I busted my ass there," she recalls. She and her husband broke up a number of times and Myrtle would return to Fredericton, but they would always patch things up and return to New Haven. He eventually left her and the children. "I had to think like both a man and a woman — had to be tough — my kids are still scared of me." She adds, "Lots of men are jackasses."

Through the years, Myrtle worked at a variety of jobs, never afraid to turn her hand to anything in order to keep her children fed. "Don't know how I did it sometimes," she says. "I felt like I was just a worker. Hospital, factory work — rain or shine — kept on going, working for my children." Back in Fredericton she was employed at the Lord Beaverbrook Hotel, washing dishes, making sandwiches, working buffets, doing anything she was instructed to do. She also worked as a housekeeper and babysitter. When she went for job interviews, she would let all the other applicants go ahead of her. She wanted to be the last one to speak to the interviewers. "I would tell them, 'This is how it is — I can't read or write. I'm a good worker. Either you want to hire me or you don't,' and a lot of times they would call me back."

Daily life was hard, but having a good memory helped. "I carried a book and pencil and drew maps for myself, memorized streets and sidewalks. For shopping I knew the basics. If I didn't know what something was, I wouldn't buy it, just got basic stuff. My mother always told me, 'Ask questions and you'll get answers.' I asked more questions than Carter has little liver pills," she smiles, "but I got answers. Thank God I speak up. I want to know things. I'm glad that I can speak English. I got along by asking questions." In restaurants Myrtle would order the same things over and over again. "I'd just ask for a hamburger or hot dog with fries. I got tired of the same things, but I couldn't read the menu."

All of Myrtle's children attended school. She would help them when they were just starting out. "I knew my *abc*'s and my numbers, and I could put letters together to spell words. I would read my kids the pictures in books, make them colour their *abc* letters and pronounce them. I tried to help them learn." She is proud of their accomplishments. "Tony and Julia were not quitters in school. They won scholarships — it opened the door to college for them. My kids struggled. I told them, don't ever give up."

Myrtle considers herself a loner. She frequently remarks that many of the people and friends she knew years ago are now dead. She loves to walk and goes for daily strolls around the neighbourhood. She has participated in three Terry Fox fundraisers. She smiles mischievously, "I saw a program about him once. He swore a lot, but people still gave him money."

In 1998-99, after many years of being too shy and hesitant to go, Myrtle attended her first adult literacy program, which was held at the Old Band Hall near her home. While this program did not last long, she did receive an achievement award for her efforts. Myrtle made a second and more successful attempt to improve her literacy skills after a knee operation. One day, while she was convalescing at the Dr. Everett Chalmers Hospital, a nurse asked her about the crayons and colouring book she carried almost everywhere she went.

The nurse said, "You colour beautifully. Do you draw?"

"No, I don't do that," Myrtle answered.

"Can you read and write?"

"No." At first the nurse was surprised; later, she gave Myrtle the phone number for the John Howard Society office in Fredericton. She told her that the organization could help her learn to read and write. Myrtle kept the number close by for months. "I held on to that number for a long time, and I kept saying I'm going to check that out some day."

When she finally did call, she had a nice chat with a woman called Lisa, who told her to come over to the office and set up an appointment. "I told her that I wouldn't like to sit in a crowded classroom, and she told me we can do this one-on-one. That made me feel better."

After her success with the John Howard Society, Myrtle became an adult learner with LLNB in 2004. She likes working with her teacher, Maureen (to whom she teaches Maliseet words), and she tackles her learning with the same tenacity that she did her working life. She is rightfully proud of the progress she has made and the recognition she has been given over the years. Myrtle is currently working her way through *Laubach Way to Reading Skills Book 3* and reading some storybooks. Her accomplishments are impressive: she is an adult learner/literacy advocate and a member of the SOUL Speakers Bureau for the LCNB. The John Howard Society of Fredericton presented her with the Harold Sharp Award in recognition of Academic Achievement in 2003. In 2005, she received one of the Literacy Coalition's Sheree Fitch Adult Leadership Scholarships. Two years later, she won the Canada Post Community Literacy Award for Individual Achievement. Myrtle and her six-year-old granddaughter Timea are pictured on the April page of the 2008 "ABC Canada Family Literacy Calendar." She has been interviewed on CBC Radio and Rogers Television. She goes into classrooms to talk to children about her experiences.

Myrtle is no longer afraid to discuss what she has been through, but when she was younger she was shy and didn't tell many people about her low literacy skills. She has a sixth sense, however, about others with the same challenges. "I often feel that something is wrong. They might be called a 'slow learner.' Usually I can tell if someone can't read or write." As well, she feels that those with literacy difficulties usually have good math skills. "I'm good at adding and taking away, always have been. I always carried a little calculator around with me. You couldn't fool my mother, Annie Paul, when it came to numbers. I notice that about people who can't read well."

Myrtle plans to continue her work with LLNB. She would like to accomplish other things, but at the moment isn't sure what they will be. She thinks she would like to try painting or some other aspect of the visual arts. Her improving reading skills have given her the confidence to tackle new challenges, to try things she never has before. Recently Myrtle attended an adult art workshop at the Beaverbrook Art Gallery, her first foray into art.

Now she and Timea, who is in grade one, help each other to read. Her granddaughter tells her to "keep studying" and "someday we might graduate together."

"She cracks me up," Myrtle says smiling proudly.

Teena's Dream
JANET HAMMOCK

At the time of writing, Teena is working with Cynthia at the CALP Centre in the Octagonal House in Sackville, New Brunswick, towards the successful completion of the GED exams. After Teena shared with me the personal goal that keeps her moving forward, I decided to situate her story in the future. Here, Teena has reached her goal and is living her dream. Mrs. Beal, while bearing a striking resemblance to several Sackville seniors, is an entirely fictional character.

"When you make house calls," the teacher had emphasized, "arrive early, sit in your car, and breathe deeply for a moment to calm your shaky hands!" Teena was glad of that advice now because her heart thumped fast and loud as she swung her Toyota into a parking place overlooking a path to the Waterfowl Park and then turned off the engine.

Here she was, a certified nail technician, about to enter a cottage at the United Church Home for Senior Citizens to do the nails of Mrs. Beal, her first professional client, about to live her dream that, just a few years ago, had seemed impossible.

She had done her own nails for years, thinking of them as manicured jewels. Sparkles were her specialty. Today, Teena had accented her shimmering nails with an enormous trendy ring of glittering stones and a watch to match. Glancing down at her hands, she felt her confidence grow. It's a great look, she thought with satisfaction. When Mrs. Beal sees my nails, she'll know I can do the job right.

Last night she'd checked her professional nail case several times to be sure she had everything she'd need. Inside the lid she'd stuck miniature copies of her CALP graduation certificate, her GED results, and her nail technician graduation diploma. Tucked around them were her favourite family photographs: "Baby" Jessica proudly walking across the high-school stage in her graduation robe and gold-tasselled mortarboard; middle son, Jason, with his laughing eyes and easygoing manner playing Final Fantasy with a buddy after work; and John, her oldest, sitting with his dad in front of the TV, watching a boxing match.

Mark's smiling face she wore in a gold locket next to her heart — the Place of Honour, he'd say with a grin. What a guy, she thought, encouraging me every year when that flyer from CALP showed up in our mailbox.

"Why don't you give it a try?" he'd suggest.

"Never, never, never!" she'd shoot back at him. "Do you think I'm crazy? Why would I want to put myself through that torture again?" And the matter would drop, until the next year.

"OK Tiger!" Teena addressed the car as she locked the doors. "You look so sweet, but *grrrrr* you can be ferocious, just like me, when you need to be! Tiger, you can do it! Here we go!" Suitcase in hand, she walked toward the white-haired woman waiting for her on the cottage porch and reached out to shake her hand. "Hi, Mrs. Beal! I'm Teena!"

Four months later . . .

One of the reasons Teena chose this line of work was that she loved to listen to her clients' stories. As a child she had always been the one her friends sought out when they were in trouble. "Go tell Teena!" they'd say to each other. "She'll know what to do!" Now she listened to women share with her intimate details about their lives. Mrs. Beal occupied a special place in Teena's heart as her first and favourite storyteller.

Today, Mrs. Beal surprised her. "Honey, you *always* listen to me! This morning I want to hear about you. Tell me about your childhood, your friends, why you dropped out of school, why you went back — I want to hear every detail!"

Teena smiled affectionately as she took Mrs. Beal's wrinkled hands in hers, placed them in a bowl of warm water, and covered it with a linen cloth. While the steam performed its healing, she began to assemble applicators and pearly polishes on the table between them.

"I have few memories from my childhood, Mrs. Beal, but there *are* a couple of things I will *never* forget. When I was very young, our house in Oshawa was situated at the bottom of a steep hill. At the top was a truck-stop restaurant. One day the brakes gave out on a huge semi that was parked up there, and it rolled down the hill and crashed through the side of our house into the living room, where my little brother and I were watching TV! I was terrified. Can you believe our mom just stayed in the kitchen and yelled out, 'What are you kids doing?' Was she drunk? I don't know . . . probably."

"Oh, my dear," Mrs. Beal murmured sympathetically as Teena, struggling to regain her usual cheerful demeanour, patted her hands dry with a soft towel. She looked forward to the next step, when Teena would apply dollops of warm oil to her hands and begin a gentle, deep massage.

"When we first moved to Sackville we lived for a short time with my Mom's parents on their wonderful homestead. I loved the old two-storey house that had so many rooms you had to go looking if you wanted to know where someone was. It was the only place my family ever lived that felt like home.

"I entered middle school, and at first it was fun, but in grade eight my math troubles began. I just couldn't get it. I could see that all my friends understood, and I felt so dumb that I dropped out. My friends missed me a lot and begged me to come back so I could go to high school with them in the fall. Finally, I went to see the principal and persuaded him to allow me to return. Somehow, I passed grade eight and the following September went off with my friends to high school.

"The new school was so huge; I felt totally overwhelmed. And I was in big trouble right away in math. It wasn't until I started CALP that I realized my problem had actually begun several grades earlier, when I was taught to subtract from left to right instead of from right to left. My tutor, Cynthia, showed me why it was impossible to get the right answers subtracting in the wrong direction.

"I also couldn't do math word problems. Although I was good in reading and writing, word problems might as well have been written in Chinese. I could not grasp them at all. Even thinking about them now gives me a horrible feeling in my gut. I'd stand in line with the other 'problem' kids to see the teacher. When my turn came he'd go *flick*, *jot*, *tick*, down my sheet, say a word or two really fast, ask if I understood, and then call out 'Next!' No remedial work or tutoring was available. I hated going to school because I always felt so bad. Finally I couldn't stand it anymore, and in grade nine I dropped out again."

"Your mom and dad allowed you to quit?"

"Oh, Mrs. Beal, you know how it is around here. My parents were partiers. Our house was a party house all the time, but especially on weekends. I dreaded weekends. At first it was only Dad who would get drunk, but later Mom drank too much, too. I might not have quit if my parents had insisted, 'You stay in school,' but they couldn't.

"Me and my school friends partied, too. Drinking and drugs were everywhere. I tried drugs, but for some reason I didn't stay with them. I don't know why, but I always had a feeling there was something different, something better out there for me.

"About that time I became best friends with Chris — she was a party girl. One day her mom and dad invited me to come live with them. Chris and I shared a very pretty room with twin beds. Those days are among my happiest early memories. I felt so safe there. They even celebrated birthdays and Christmas! I have no memory of birthday parties or presents in my family when I was a child. After a while, Chris and I made a pact to be different from the other kids and stop the drinking. I managed to do it, but Chris couldn't. She already had a serious problem. I tried to help her, but nothing worked. Finally I moved back home again."

"How difficult it must have been for you to return, Teena, especially leaving your best friend behind. You must have felt very lonely." Mrs. Beal's understanding words spoke directly to Teena's heart. "What did you do all day long?"

"Well, I worked a little around the house and got odd jobs here and there. One was at the Shell station in Aulac. Because I was still living at home, it was a real problem for me to get back at night. Dad would usually drive me to work, but I could not rely on him to pick me up. One night I was so angry at him for being too drunk to come get me and so upset with my mother for not keeping him from drinking, that I ended up walking back to Sackville alone in the dark on the Trans-Can."

Mrs. Beal's heart ached for this lovely woman as she listened to her story. She watched as Teena gently pushed back her softened cuticles and applied a light lavender base coat to each nail. While the polish was drying, she and Teena looked over bottle after bottle of lustrous pastels, finally choosing a delicate mauve pearl and a sheer topcoat of silver sparkle to finish.

"Soon after, I moved to Fredericton with a few friends and tried to find work there. It turned out to be just another party scene, and I came home after six months. Then all my friends decided to 'go out West' to work, and I went with them. What a trip that turned out to be! Our crummy old car broke down on the way, and we had to leave it behind and finish the trip by bus.

"Life was a struggle in Calgary, but one good thing happened. I met my husband-to-be. Mark was a Sackvillian, too, but I had never met him here. He had a good job in Calgary and was a great boxer — he won the Canadian Lightweight Championship! Neither of us wanted the party lifestyle we'd fallen into, despite our best efforts to resist. I said 'Mark, let's go home to Sackville and leave this behind forever!' And we did.

"We soon married and started a family. I decided to stay at home to raise the kids right. After they were in school, I worked different jobs here and there. At my last job in the Salvation Army Store, I had a great boss, Vicki, who had real confidence in my abilities and gave me the freedom to try out new things. I began to take initiative, improving the store in lots of ways."

Having finished applying a final sheen of silver sparkles, Teena relaxed back in her chair.

"At that point I had never considered going back to school. Not having math skills didn't present a problem in my daily life. I'm smart and had figured out on my own how to do basic stuff like balance my chequebook. My reading and writing skills were good. But one day something happened that changed everything."

"Oh, no!"cried Mrs. Beal. "Everything sounds perfect! What happened?"

"Don't worry, Mrs. Beal!" Teena hastened to reassure her friend. "I might not have mentioned that during those 'perfect' years I had seriously wrenched my back several times. I'd be put on workers' compensation, suffer through weeks of pain and physio treatments, and then go right back into the same type of job. One day I walked down the Salvation Army Store aisle, my arms piled high with clothes, and tripped over a farm set some kid had left on the floor. Clothes flew every which way, and when I hit the floor, I felt my back go again. The handwriting was on the wall! I simply couldn't do that type of work any longer.

"Amy, one of my co-workers, was a trained nail technician and had taught me everything she knew. She thought I had a special talent for doing nails and urged me again to enrol in the course.

"With my back throbbing in pain, I drove straight to the Employment Insurance office and asked what I needed to qualify for the nail course. I had to be a high school graduate or pass the GED exams, the woman told me, and she suggested it would be financially helpful if I were laid off from my job. The next week, when my boss was trying to decide who to lay off, I volunteered and explained why. She was very encouraging and supportive of my decision.

"The next step, they said, would be to write EI tests in every subject to determine my grade level because I had to complete grade nine successfully before I could start preparing for my GEDs. When I heard the word 'tests,' I got the same horrible sinking feeling in my gut that I used to have in school. But Mark reminded me that I'm a real fighter and my desire to upgrade was stronger than my fear, so I took the test, and just as I suspected, my math skills tested out at around a grade five level. In every other subject I was at the grade nine level, except in English, where I achieved a grade ten! I felt extremely encouraged by my test results."

"I should think so!" Mrs. Beal smiled broadly.

"Upgrading in math was arranged with Cynthia. I was apprehensive about going to the CALP Centre, but I liked Cynthia as soon as I met her and began to feel less scared. She gave me her own test in math to determine where we needed to start work together. We began with basic arithmetic — adding, subtracting, and so on — and almost immediately she discovered the little hole that had led to my downfall in school. Imagine! One small, misunderstood subtracting skill was responsible for all those years of grief."

"My goodness! I'm glad Cynthia was able to help. But tell me, Teena, how did it feel to go back to school as an adult?"

"It was completely different — much, much better! My classes started early each morning and lasted four hours. In the Centre, I was surrounded by people working to upgrade their skills. Cynthia spent as much time with each of us as we needed. She was amazing. I'd never had a teacher like her. She would sit beside me, and we would go over my mistakes together and find out exactly where I'd gone wrong. At first, when I didn't understand what Cynthia was talking about, I would feel dreadful. Cynthia told me later that she could see the panic in my eyes. Gradually, I began to trust that when I didn't understand her explanation I could tell her so. She would calmly reply: 'OK. You don't understand it that way. Let's try this way.' What wonderful patience she had."

"You finally found a healthy learning environment." Mrs. Beal sighed with relief.

"That's for sure. A surprising door opened for me at CALP: I could actually 'get' math because I was being taught right. What a high!" Teena's face shone. "I'm lucky. When my family wasn't there for me as a kid, I was forced to become independent and found ways to cope. The fact that I could be there for my school friends also helped. Several people have said to me that I'd be a great counsellor! Maybe they're right! I love telling people what to do!"

Teena and Mrs. Beal burst into laughter. Laughter is always around when

Teena's here, Mrs. Beal thought. Whoever said a good belly laugh is better than a thousand pills was certainly right.

While she watched Teena pack her kit to leave, Mrs. Beal realized she felt much happier than earlier in the day, when she'd been rather despondent about her limited life in the nursing home cottage. She was filled with deep admiration for this attractive woman who had helped her so much by sharing her own life. Mrs. Beal sensed that she had helped Teena in some important way, too.

After giving Mrs Beal a warm hug goodbye, Teena placed her suitcase on the back seat of the car and walked down the grassy slope to the path that led through bushes and trees to the Waterfowl Park. She'd noticed this path many times before but had never thought to walk on it until today.

This is just like my returning to school, she mused, enjoying the deep autumn colours, still blooming rose bushes, and wild apple trees along the way. The path to upgrade my education was always there, but until I had a good reason to set foot on it, I hardly noticed it. Who would have thought that a bad back and an exciting dream would carry me along on this path? The world is a good place to be, Teena thought, as she turned, once again, towards home.

Afterword: Adventures in Literacy
GREG COOK

These portraits of adult learners, whose beginnings were potentially tragic, are, as one writer calls her subject, "an inspiration." For this I thank the storytellers — for their brave leadership in sharing their stories so others might receive "rights they're entitled to" in our society.

The writers' discoveries of different journeys — from the fearful isolation of illiteracy to the empowerment of literacy — have a common message. The stigmas society often attaches to "illiterates" are false.

Labelled as "stupid" or "retarded" or treated as if they had a "disease," the literacy-challenged have more than poor schooling to hurdle. Their paths to literacy begin with overcoming the fear of asking for help. Frequently first treated as "special needs" learners, their segregation becomes a disincentive.

These are stories of people who conquered their fears and were creative enough to think outside the boxes in which they found themselves. In so doing they have discovered ways to "transform lives" — their own and those of family members and friends. With this book, they are helping to transform the lives of others.

When I heard of this project, I immediately thought of my old friend Alden Nowlan (1933-1983), who dropped out of school in Nova Scotia before completing grade five. He came to New Brunswick as a young adult and became one of Canada's — and the world's — outstanding poets. Interestingly, the first biography of Alden Nowlan was written by Stacy Howroyd as a reader for new literates and was published by the Literacy Council of Fredericton the year after Nowlan died.

Alden was born into a broken family disadvantaged by poverty and alcoholism. He learned to read and write early — write so early and so well, in fact, that once when he turned in an essay the teacher sent him home from school as punishment for what she thought was plagiarism. His "special needs" isolated him. He, like imaginative new readers in this book, "pretended" to be in special places in his mind through his reading and writing.

For some time, Alden worked on a story about a kind of fantasy world; although he never published it. The hero was an uneducated, young goat-herder who rose to legislative power and reformed his country's education system. What Alden's hero wished for is the kind of world the literacy organizations listed in this book hope for.

Of course, Alden never had to polish and publish his fantasy story. Instead he published a poem which may say it all. He turned his loneliness and the school system's failure of him into a kind of miracle adventure called "A Boy in a Red Loin Cloth." In the poem men bring him a "beautiful white horse" to ride through the jungle where "pygmies would suddenly emerge from the trees" to take him like a prisoner along a "secret road to the city." There he would be made a brother by "a house of children,"

> and in time he would leave there, but by then he would know
> so many singular arts all men would be awed by him, and
>   whenever he wished
> he would
> summon the beautiful white horse and ride back to the jungle. [†]

This is a fantasy. The reality is that Alden read, and was read to, as a pre-schooler. Many of us have become, and future readers will become, "awed" by his accomplishments. Primarily because, like the tellers in these pages, he had the "confidence to stand up and tell" his own story.

We should also know Alden would agree, as one of the speakers says, "Whoever said a good belly laugh is better than a thousand pills was certainly

---

[†]   Alden Nowlan, "A Boy in a Red Loin Cloth," in *Bread, Wine and Salt* (Toronto: Clarke, Irwin & Company Limited, 1967), p.65.

right!" He laughed at himself, and so he laughed at the Canadian government in the 1970s, when Statistics Canada reported anyone who had not finished grade eight was "functionally illiterate."

He never laughed, however, at the struggle of those who could not read or write. In his poem, "Incident Observed While Picking Up the Mail," he notices a vulnerable eight-year-old and a man. The two are in "bib overalls and rubber boots," and "out of the corner of my eye I watch / the boy sign the man's name / to an unemployment insurance cheque." The poet is tempted to follow them across the street and into the bank:

> so that I can see them smile
> at one another, lovingly,
> as the cashier examines
> the signature and finds it good.
> Father and son — it would be impossible
> to decide which of them is the prouder.[‡]

‡   Alden Nowlan, "Incident Observed While Picking Up the Mail" in *I'm a Stranger Here Myself* (Toronto/ Vancouver: Clarke, Irwin & Company Limited, 1974), p.54.

Appendices

The appendices are comprised of three parts: a statistical summary, adult learning program information in New Brunswick, and contact information for literacy service providers in New Brunswick and elsewhere in Canada.

Appendix 1
Adult Literacy Statistics

In 2003, the International Adult Literacy and Skills Survey (IALSS) tested more than twenty-three thousand Canadians on their proficiency in four literacy domains.

Literacy Domains:
Prose literacy: reading continuous text such as the sort found in books, newspaper articles, brochures, and instruction manuals
Document literacy: reading text that is not continuous such as the sort contained in graphs, charts, payroll forms, and job applications
Numeracy: math skills
Problem solving: analytical reasoning
Literacy Proficiency Levels:
    Level 1: have few basic skills, great deal of difficulty with text.
    Level 2: have limited skills, cannot read well, can deal only with
            material that is simply and clearly laid out.
    Level 3: have a basic skill level but may have problems with more

complex tasks. Level 3 is considered the minimum skill level
for successful participation in society.

Levels 4 and 5: have high levels of literacy with a wide range of reading
skills and many strategies for dealing with complex materials.
Individuals at these levels can meet most reading demands and
can handle new reading challenges.

Results

The following table shows the percentage of adults (over sixteen years of age)
from east coast to west coast who scored in Levels 1 and 2 (below minimum skill
level) in 2003.

Province/Territory	Prose literacy	Document literacy	Numeracy	Problem solving
Newfoundland and Labrador	55	58	65	81
Prince Edward Island	50	51	60	77
Nova Scotia	45	47	57	74
New Brunswick	56	58	65	81
Québec	55	57	59	76
Ontario	48	49	56	76
Manitoba	46	47	56	72
Saskatchewan	40	41	49	69
Alberta	40	40	49	67
British Columbia	40	40	49	66
Nunavut	73	74	78	89
Northwest Territories	45	46	53	72
Yukon	33	36	43	63
Canada	48	49	55	76

Appendix 2
Programs in New Brunswick

Community Adult Learning Programs (CALPs)
The Government of New Brunswick (GNB) provides basic skills learning through its CALP network. The objective of the program is to improve literacy levels in the province by bringing literacy training opportunities to adults in their own communities. This program is open to adult learners eighteen years of age and over. The program is offered free of charge.

In this program, adult learners can obtain instruction in English or French. Academic services for grade levels one through nine and GED preparation are accessible in seventy communities throughout the province. Programs are customized for individual learner's needs. The program offers a standardized curriculum and testing providing accreditation for further study. Learners who complete GED preparation go on to take the GED exam.

The program is delivered through a network of community-based centres, is group-based, and requires a learner commitment of approximately thirty hours per week. Teachers use a standard curriculum that incorporates both literacy and numeracy. Initial assessment guides the placement of the individual learner to a particular level/resource starting point. Progress through the curriculum would be recorded as learners advance. Teachers within the program are paid staff.

In addition to the CALP programs, GNB has developed a competency-based Workplace Essential Skills program aimed at helping adults gain the skills necessary to find and keep employment. This is a relatively new program and is only offered in a limited number of locations.

Laubach Literacy New Brunswick (LLNB)
Laubach Literacy has been in Canada since the first tutor-training workshop was held in Lunenburg County, Nova Scotia, in 1970. In the few years following that session, several literacy councils, all located in the eastern provinces, were formed. The first Laubach council in New Brunswick was established in Saint John in 1975.

After more than a decade of pioneering work, LLNB was formed in 1983. The provincial office for Laubach Literacy is located in Moncton and is staffed by a full-time executive director.

Currently there are fifteen Laubach Literacy councils/community contact points in New Brunswick operating with approximately five hundred tutors and volunteers. The councils are situated in the following locations:

Bathurst	Fredericton	Port Elgin
Campbellton	Fundy	Sackville
Carleton	Grand Manan	Saint John
Dorchester	Keswick Valley	Sussex
Westmorland	Miramichi	
Florenceville	Moncton	

LLNB is a registered, non-profit charitable organization. All of its income is derived from donations and grants. Through its provincial office and fifteen affiliated literacy councils and community contact points, LLNB trains and certifies volunteer tutors to help New Brunswick adults and youth learn literacy and numeracy skills through a free, confidential program. LLNB programs are offered in English only.

Although most of the training has been focused on adults at literacy proficiency Levels 1 and 2, LLNB has also provided language training to hundreds of immigrants and has established peer youth literacy tutoring programs in schools.

LLNB's program is flexible and designed to meet the individual student's needs. Laubach resources are broken down into different levels so that learners can start at a level appropriate to their current skills. A combination of resources is used, including the original "Each One Teach One" method.

The program is private and the students and tutors meet at mutually convenient times and locations. The length of each session and the duration of the program are tailored to meet the specific requirements of the student.

Appendix 3
Literacy Service Providers across Canada

The following is a list of contact information for literacy service providers (English) that begins with the province in which this book originated and then moves into an alphabetical nationwide list by province and territory.

In New Brunswick:
   Laubach Literacy New Brunswick: Provincial Office (Executive Director)
   Telephone 1-877-633-8899 or 1-506-384-6371
   websitewww.nald.ca/llnb

   Community Adult Learning Network
   Telephone 1-877-444-0510
   website www.cnbb.nb.ca/en/english.htm

Community Adult Learning Coordinators' telephone numbers:
   Miramichi Region 1-506-778-5261
   Moncton Region 1-506-856-2241
   South-West Region 1-506-658-6701
   Woodstock Region 1-506-325-4866

The Writers' Federation of New Brunswick (WFNB) has provided support and services to New Brunswick writers since its incorporation in 1985. Striv-ing to create a community of writers, it is open to any individual interested in writing. Its membership includes new and emerging writers and community memoirists as well as mid-career professionals and internationally acclaimed authors. The WFNB promotes the works of New Brunswick writers, provides educational services to schools and libraries, sponsors readings, book launches, workshops, and an annual Canada-wide literary competition.

Contact WFNB:
    Telephone 1-506-459-7228
    Email wfnb@nb.aibn.com
    Website www.umce.ca/wfnb

Elsewhere in Canada:

ALBERTA
    Community Learning Network
    #4 10012-29A Avenue
    Edmonton, AB, T6N 1A8
    Telephone 1-780-485-4926 or 485-4921 or toll free 1-877-485-4926

    The Further Education Society of Alberta
    #52-3033 34th Avenue Northeast
    Calgary, AB, T1Y 6X2
    Telephone 1-403-350-5034

    Literacy Alberta
    3060-17 Avenue SW
    Calgary, AB, T3E 7G8
    Telephone 1-403-410-6990

BRITISH COLUMBIA
    Literacy B.C.
    601-510 West Hastings Street
    Vancouver, BC, V6B 1L8
    Telephone 1-604-684-0624 or toll free 1-888-732-3234

    Readnow BC
    Ministry of Education
    P.O. Box 9161 Stn Provincial Government
    Victoria, BC, V8W 9H3
    Telephone 1-250-387-7097 or toll free hotline 1-888-732-3234

MANITOBA
 Manitoba Advanced Education & Literacy, Adult Literacy and Learning
 350-800 Portage Avenue
 Winnipeg, MB, R3G 0N4
 Telephone 1-204-945-8247

 Literacy Partners of Manitoba
 401-321 McDermot Avenue
 Winnipeg, MB, R3A 0A3
 Telephone 1-204-947-5757 or toll free 1-866-947-5757

NEWFOUNDLAND & LABRADOR
 Literacy in Newfoundland & Labrador
 Suite 205 2nd Floor Fall River Plaza
 272-276 Torbay Road
 St. John's, NL, A1A 4E1
 Telephone 1-709-738-7323 or toll free 1-800-563-1111

 Newfoundland & Labrador Laubach Literacy Council
 141 O'Connell Drive
 P.O. Box 822
 Corner Brook, NL, A2H 6H6
 Telephone 1-709-634-5081 or toll free 1-800-863-0373

NORTHWEST TERRITORIES
 Northwest Territories Literacy Council
 Box 761, 5122-48th Street
 Yellowknife, NT, X1A 2N6
 Telephone 1-867-873-9262 or toll free 1-866-599-6758

NOVA SCOTIA

Laubach Literacy of Nova Scotia
28 Hillview Street, South End Community Centre
Sydney, NS, B1P 6J9
Telephone 1-902-564-8404

Literacy Nova Scotia
P.O. Box 1516
Truro, NS, B2N 3V2
Telephone1-902-897-2444 or toll free 1-800-255-5203

NUNAVUT

Nunavut Literacy Council
Box 1049
Cambridge Bay, NU, X0B 0C0
Telephone toll free 1-866-608-2678

ONTARIO

Laubach Literacy Ontario
8A-65 Noecker Street
Waterloo, ON, N2J 2R6
Telephone 1-519-743-3309 or toll free 1-866-608-2574

Ontario Literacy Coalition
65 Wellesley Street East, Suite 503
Toronto, ON, M4Y 1G7
Telephone 1-416-963-5787

PRINCE EDWARD ISLAND

Laubach Literacy PEI
Field Services Coordinator
Telephone 1-902-964-2883 or 1-902-621-2824
Reading line toll free 1-800-348-7323

PEI Literacy Alliance
P.O. Box 20107
Charlottetown, PE, C1A 9E3
Telephone 1-902-368-3620

QUEBEC (English)
Literacy in Action
257 Queen Street
Sherbrook, QC, J1M 1K7
Telephone 1-819-346-7009 or toll free 1-888-303-7009

Literacy Volunteers of Quebec
153 Sugar Hill Road
Lac-Brome, QC, J0E 1V0
Telephone 1-450-243-5346 or toll free 1-866-581-9512

SASKATCHEWAN
Saskatchewan Literacy Network
202-626 Broadway Avenue
Saskatoon, SK, S7N 1A9
Telephone 1-306-651-7288 or toll free 1-888-511-2111

Saskatchewan Ministry of Education
Literacy Office
4th Floor, 2220 College Avenue
Regina, SK, S4P 4V9
Telephone 1-306-787-2514

YUKON
Yukon Learn Society
107 Main Street
Whitehorse, YT, Y1A 1Y6
Telephone 1-867-668-6280 or toll free 1-888-668-6280

The Yukon Literacy Coalition
207-200 Main Street
Whitehorse, YT, Y1A 2A8
Telephone 1-867-668-6535

Please note: The toll free numbers apply only in their respective provinces/
territories.

Contributors

JUDY BOWMAN's poetry and prose have appeared in *Room, Qwerty, The Vagrant Revue of New Fiction, Rattle,* and *Bread n' Molasses.* As a journalist with the *Miramichi Leader*, she often features stories about family violence and the effects of residential schools on First Nation's people. In 2009, her readers honoured her with the *Miramichi Leader*'s Readers' Choice Award for Favourite Journalist.

NOELINE BRIDGE writes mostly non-fiction and has published a number of articles and book chapters, some in her professional field of indexing books. Her non-fiction has twice won first prize in the Writers Federation of New Brunswick literary competitions. She co-authored *Royals of England: A Guide for Readers, Travelers, and Genealogists* and is compiling a book on indexing names, to be published in 2010.

EVELYN BUTCHER lives in Miramichi, New Brunswick. She is a two-time open-heart surgery survivor, mother, homemaker, and a member of the Writers Federation of New Brunswick. The *Miramichi Leader* has published her articles and stories, and she has served as editor of her church newsletter for several years. She completed with highest honours a comprehensive Freelance Writer Course through International Correspondence School and attended four times the week-long Maritime Writers Workshop at UNB.

GREG COOK lives in Saint John, New Brunswick. His biography *One Heart, One Way / Alden Nowlan: A Writer's Life* was published by Pottersfield Press. His latest book of poetry, *Songs of the Wounded: new and selected poems,* was published by

Black Moss. He edited *Alden Nowlan: Essays on His Works* for Guernica Editions. He is currently writing a biography of another friend, novelist Ernest Buckler, whose novel *The Mountain and the Valley* is a seminal Canadian classic.

RICHARD DOIRON, a vocal human rights activist, has worked in print for forty-five years. Author of seventeen books, including two novels and two biographical works, he has been twice nominated for the Governor General's Award and has won international literary competitions. Twice published in forums with the Dalai Lama by invitation, his work has also been read at the United Nations and at the World Congress of Poetry & Cultures. His main themes are spirituality and peace.

LAURIE GLENN NORRIS lives in Lower Kingsclear, New Brunswick, with her husband Barry. She is currently employed with the Beaverbrook Art Gallery. Her first book, *Cumberland County, Facts and Folklore*, was recently published. She thanks Myrtle for sharing her experiences and her wisdom.

KATHIE GOGGIN is a member of Fredericton's Wilmot Writers. She is grateful to her mother who read bedtime stories to her, to her grade one teacher who taught her to read phonetically, to her sisters who shared her love of reading and who helped lug home library books by wagon in the summer and by toboggan in the winter, and mostly to her daughters who sat quietly on her lap while being read to.

JANET HAMMOCK is a Vancouver-born concert pianist who holds both Master and Doctor of Musical Arts degrees from Yale University. She was a professor of music for thirty-one years, first at Whittier College in California and then at Mount Allison University, where, after retirement, she was appointed Professor Emeritus of Music. Recently, Janet returned to creative writing, something she has enjoyed since childhood. She and her partner live in Sackville, New Brunswick, with Loofa, their sixteen-year-old cat.

JUNE HORSMAN is a grandmother and hobby writer who lives in Moncton, New Brunswick. She has had some poems and short stories published. Her favourite request is when one of her grandchildren says; "'Tell us a story," and she can.

AFIENA KAMMINGA is inspired by the way her dog, Wibo, snatches his indestructible canine Frisbee in mid-flight and proceeds to worry the captive rubber disk to within an inch of its Frisbee life, convinced that one day it will reveal all its secrets, yes, the very essence of its Frisbee-ness to him. Afiena doggedly worries words and phrases — in two languages to double the fun — in her lifelong quest to become the best (re-)writer she can be.

WENDY KITTS is a freelance writer, artist, and graphic designer based in Moncton, New Brunswick, who believes that everybody has a story, and the favourite part of her job is unearthing that story — whether by pen, by brush, or by mouse. Wendy's articles have appeared in *The Beaver*, the *Globe & Mail*, *More*, and *Saltscapes*. To learn more about Wendy's story and her company, Communications by Design, go to www.wendykitts.ca.

CAROL KNEPPER retired from teaching English and began writing poems focusing on the themes of nature, spirituality, and humanitarianism. She has read at local, national, and international events and has been aired on CBC. Her poems have been published in Richard Vallance's *Canadian Zen Haiku*, Sondra Ball's *Autumn Leaves,* and displayed several times at the World Poetry Project of Vancouver, British Columbia. Her books of poetry include *Clean And Simple Stones*, *My World of Etherées*, and *My Ink Exposed*.

MARILYN LERCH, who lives in Sackville, New Brunswick, has one cycle of poems and two collections of poetry published. She enters her seventh decade still asking the big questions, still wondering what our species is turning into, as excited by mourning doves nesting in the kiwi as she is by Hubble's farthest reach.

BETH POWNING is the author of four books: *Seeds of Another Summer*, *Shadow Child*, *The Hatbox Letters*, and *Edge Seasons*. She has published photography, essays, and articles in books, magazines, and anthologies. She lives near Sussex, New Brunswick, with her husband, artist Peter Powning. Her new novel is due in 2010.

ANGELA RANSON is a high-school English teacher and a Master of Arts student at Dalhousie University in Halifax, Nova Scotia. Her short stories have appeared in *Canadian Stories* magazine and *Angels on Earth* magazine and her non-fiction articles have appeared in several newspapers in the province, including the Moncton *Times and Transcript*. She is also writing scripts and recently wrote and directed a sold-out dinner theatre in Sackville, New Brunswick, entitled *Spice of Life*.

RICHARD TOTH and his wife Brenda live in Bathurst, New Brunswick. Richard's poetry has been published in a number of literary journals, and he has won prizes from the Atlantic Writing competition, the Ontario Poetry Society, and the Writers Federation of New Brunswick. He has had articles published in *The New Brunswick Reader* and in *Our Canada* magazine. His short story "Tom and Theresa" was included in the *New Brunswick Short Stories* anthology (Neptune Publishing, 2003).

DAWN WATSON is a writer who has been blessed to be a Laubach tutor. She has been able to see Felicia grow into a special young lady, and has benefitted by the humour, stamina, and goodness of her student.

LAURA WELLS is very pleased to be able to contribute to this project. Laura really values education; she returned to university as a mature student. Previously, she worked in the field of education as an elementary school teacher and as a teacher of English as a Second Language. She now works as a freelance writer and divides her time between Atlantic Canada and the United States.